Real Stories From Real Teenagers

BEING A BETTER HUMAN TEENAGER

Better Humans in Progress
Steve Brierley, MA, CEC
Melissa From, CFRE
Paul Lamoureux, MA, CEC
Hillary Rideout, CPHR, BHRM

Tellwell Talent
www.tellwell.ca

ISBN
978-0-2288-3925-5 (Paperback)
978-0-2288-3926-2 (eBook)

Table of Contents

Foreword

Welcome to our team's very first book! We really wanted to create something inspirational. We aimed for a book that showcases teenagers who are really making a difference in their home, school, and communities. A book that all teenagers would read and say, "I can do that too!" A book that would show how much of a difference just one teenager can make, and provide all teenagers with a source of motivation to do the same, wherever they are.

Our entire team consists of parents. We are all deeply inspired to help our kids be successful, and we are all committed to showing our children how important it is to do something that makes a positive difference on a daily basis. We want this book to make a difference in your life too. We want you to see this book as a tool for being a Better Human and to introduce you to a new way of thinking: "How can I be better every day?"

In the hunt for inspiring stories, we searched for normal teenagers - just like you - who are making a big difference in the world every day, to show you just how simple it really is to be a Better Human Teenager. We conducted numerous interviews with teenagers and asked questions that would bring out their very best thoughts. We hope you are inspired by their words.

This book is divided into two parts; an inspirational story book showcasing teenagers who are just like you and who are making a difference every day, plus a journal for you to record your thoughts and plans. The first half of the book contains the research and inspiring stories that we compiled. When you flip the book over, you will find the journal. The journal serves as a place for you to write your thoughts and outline your plans and progress towards being a Better Human Teenager. The journal is intended to keep you on track and serve as a source of exploration for your thoughts; it's your accountability partner. We want you to write your thoughts, your dreams, your plans and feelings, documenting how you're becoming a Better Human Teenager every day.

From our families to yours, we hope you never forget this book. We hope that the words impact you in a way that inspires you to become better every day. We wrote it with the hope that it makes a difference and ignites a spark within you to stand out and lead the way. We truly believe in our children and want the same for them when they read this book. Together, we can create a community where we all make a difference, and today, that starts with you.

With gratitude,
Steve, Melissa, Paul, Hillary

Gratitude

This book would not be possible if it weren't for the great teenagers (and their parents) we have met through our interviews, conversations and survey. The stories have had a tremendous impact on us as authors. We have been known to shed a few tears as we learn of the inspiring work these young people are doing. Unfortunately, current media focuses heavily on all the bad things going on with youth. Rarely do we hear about all the great things going on. We think it's time to change that focus and highlight the great things our youth are doing. They are showing us how to make the world a better place. It's time we listen.

When we set out to write this book, we decided to take a methodical approach in gathering the information. We began our research with a survey; respondents were teenagers, parents, teachers, coaches, and anyone who has teens in their life. We immediately knew that we had to tell some of the stories we were hearing.

So, as a group of authors, interviewers, surveyors and passionate, imperfect people trying to be Better Humans ourselves, we would like to extend special gratitude to:

- The phenomenal teenagers who shared their stories - your willingness to share some of the most personal details of your life blows us away. You have inspired so many already and this is just the beginning of your "ripple effect."

- All the great teenagers we have not met yet, but who are making a positive difference in the world by giving back and showing compassion and caring for your fellow humans.
- The parents of the teens we interviewed - we are honoured by the trust you placed in us to tell your child's story.
- All of our own families who saw the value in this project, encouraged us to write this book and supported us along the way. It feels amazing to have a team of cheerleaders holding us up.

We hope you enjoy this book and you find something in it that inspires you to go out and be a Better Human!

Research and Insights

Our Research Approach

The idea behind this project was hatched in late 2019 during some informal coffee chats about a shared desire to make a difference and to inspire others to do the same. We bantered about what it means to be a Better Human and the discussions evolved to include debate about *who* we wanted to impact. For a multitude of reasons, we landed on teenagers being our first target.

The goal was to write a book focused on real data and include real stories of real teenagers doing Better Human kinds of things. We wanted to understand what makes these exceptional humans tick; what is it inside of them that drives them to behave in ways that better the world around them? Why do they do what they do? We wanted to inspire our readers to follow in their footsteps and build daily Better Human *practice* into their lives. What we didn't want was an academic review of literature or a recall of our own teenage years... that could have been a little scary! Our approach followed these steps:

1. We designed and developed a survey to capture relevant data about being a Better Human Teenager, such as: What does it mean to be a Better Human Teenager? Why is it important? What is the impact on others? How does it have an impact on day to day life? We focused on

gathering the data by asking open-ended questions so as not to lead anyone's responses.

2.   We sent the survey to our network and distributed it further through social media platforms like LinkedIn, Instagram and Facebook.

3.   We had a good response rate and we have kept the survey open as an ongoing desire to gather more information.

4.   We compiled the survey response data and identified themes and key concepts.

5.   In the following pages, we share our own commentary on the data and have included many of the comments from the survey.

As you will see, we gathered some great insight about what it means to be a Better Human Teenager, which is supported by the incredible stories we compiled from our interviews. Please take your time reading the comments. You will discover some interesting messages and insights.

Please enjoy what we offer in the following pages; take note of the nuggets of inspiration you uncover and think about how you can work them into your own life!

What does it mean to be a Better Human?

A common definition of what it means to be a Better Human doesn't exist, so we asked everyone and anyone who would listen, what it meant to them. In both the survey we conducted, and the interviews shared in this book, we asked what words people use to describe a Better Human Teenager. Although we heard strong themes that aren't surprising, we also heard unexpected words to describe it. It seems that it means something slightly different for everyone.

What we heard was both validating and eye opening. Many people used commonly thought of adjectives like respectful, empathetic and compassionate. Of the 124 distinct words offered in the survey, *kind* was the most commonly shared by far. It's not surprising, but it's incredibly touching to realize that kindness is all it takes for others to experience someone as a Better Human. It can be as simple as that - be kind. Isn't that powerful in its simplicity?

The word that stood out most to us was *empathetic*. Empathy was the most common concept that our interviewees used to explain what exists inside of them that drives them to do wonderful things for others. Some didn't know how to explain it, but when we got them talking, it was empathy that they were describing, just using different words. It makes so much sense! Having the ability to imagine and understand what someone else is experiencing, and act accordingly, very likely results in the recipient receiving exactly what they need when they need it.

Other words that made us smile and nod were courage, bravery, humbleness, joyful, happy, playful, resilient, inclusive, sincere, connected to what they feel matters... all very powerful ways to describe what being a Better Human Teenager is all about.

Others offered insights that we, the authors, hadn't come up with ourselves. Words like visionary, curious and forgiving were suggested. It's especially interesting to think about why these words come to mind for some of our survey respondents and interviewees. We may never know for sure, but we offer some insights.

Forgiving is the word that strikes the most curious chord. What makes the ability to forgive an attribute of someone who others view as a Better Human? On the surface, it's not obvious. But from some of the stories we heard, forgiveness plays a big part in why they do what they do. Some of those to whom we spoke have lived a life of challenge and negativity. They have heroically risen above their unfortunate pasts and have forgiven those who did them wrong. They attribute this ability to forgive to going on to live a life of giving back and helping others who are in or who have come from similarly tough pasts.

A fascinating point to ponder is the idea that being selfless is actually *selfish*. Think about it. Most of us who do kind, compassionate things for others, experience an amazing feeling. It feels good to help others. Now we're not suggesting that Better Humans do wonderful things *only* because of how it makes *them* feel, or for the kudos and "likes" they get on social media, but is doing kind things just a little selfish? Maybe. But in the best way!

What was the first word you thought of when you heard the term Better Human? Was it one of the ones we talked about, or something different?

For a complete list of the words we heard, see page 181 and 182.

What impact would a Better Human Teenager have on their school?

One of the key things we wanted to ensure was that any research we conducted could be used in the real world. After some lengthy discussions, we wondered what the impact would be in specific areas, if teenagers were doing things to help others.

The first area we wondered about was school. This really is the "so what?" about the book. It's great to talk about what people do, but adding the understanding of the result makes it real. We made it simple with this question. Teens spend a substantial amount of time at school and we knew that asking about school specifically would provide valuable insight. It turns out we were right. There is some great information in the following pages from teens, parents, coaches and teachers about the impact a Better Human Teenager could have on a school. To be transparent, we have not edited the comments, but we did put the information through spell check. We value realness, not perfection. Enjoy!

Comments from Teenagers

Depending on what the teenager would do, they could bring awareness to a cause or have an eye-opening impact on their peers.

Will become a more collaborative, communicative, and affectionate environment with active students.

Create a healthier, safer environment for friends and peers.

A Better Human Teenager would get involved with school leadership opportunities. In addition, they would volunteer in school events or school-sponsored events. Or, they would participate in school clubs and teams, in order to leave behind a positive legacy.

Actively trying to create a safe space for all their peers and schoolmates.

They would promote a positive school culture and advocate for their student body when needed, as well as helping others feel included.

Making others feel like there is someone they can turn to as a friend, encouraging people to do well in their studies and everyday life, and being able to make anyone smile.

Have a better learning environment that can make anyone feel safe and happy to be there.

Helping others out if they require it. Being enthusiastic and raising school spirit.

They would focus on their own goals at school, not judge others for their choices, and look out for people who are less fortunate or hurting. For example if someone is being bullied or isolated, they may choose to offer help or companionship.

Help students in need and encourage others to do the same.

Participating in clubs and activities, winning competitions on behalf of their school, and having a leadership role within the student body.

Helps out people whenever they can, stand up for what's right and what's wrong.

They would help make a better living environment for all and make the school a better place overall.

They would talk to new people and make everyone feel welcome, creating a more welcoming school environment.

Make school a place of learning and curiosity. All opinions are heard and thought about.

They could make school feel like a better place for many other students.

They would be able to bring all types of people together and interact with others with no judgment or hostility.

Brightening up the days of not only their peers, but also staff and faculty.

They would be a positive example among their peers.

Comments from Parents, Teachers & Coaches

Positive role modelling, mentoring, be an advocate for those who have trouble speaking out/up.

Better grades and less attention to the petty, materialistic parts of school.

Inclusiveness.

Will become a more collaborative, communicative, and affectionate environment with active students.

Create a healthier, safer environment for friends and peers.

Actively trying to create a safe space for all their peers and schoolmates.

They would promote a positive school culture and advocate for their student body when needed, as well as helping others feel included.

Increased tolerance of others. Potential to unlock new insights through creativity. Ability to push through difficulty and build emotional, intellectual, psychological, social "muscles".

Through modelling, help to create a more accepting and kind community of teenagers. "To be cool is To be kind" mentality. Unified BHTs can have a positive impact on bullying and exclusion, etc. and overall mental health.

They would be a beacon to everyone in the school, actively fight bully mentality, participate in all sorts of activities (regardless of cool or not), be kind to teachers, bus drivers, janitors.

They would be leaders.

I'm so impressed by today's youth and the action they are taking in their communities and in the world. There are so many examples and yet most stories go untold. By sharing it will inspire others to take on a new way of thinking and living, spread positivity and creative thinking.

What impact would a Better Human Teenager have on their community?

Hopefully you enjoyed reading some of the comments about the impact being a Better Human Teeneager would have on schools. Continuing in that spirit, we thought the next best place to ask about was in the community. With so much discussion about the importance of community and the wellbeing of teens, we thought it would be interesting to segment this out and get some specific comments.

You may see some repetition with the school comments but there are subtle differences. We found through our interviews that some teens are focused on their schools and some have branched out to their local community in an effort to make it a better place. Once again, we have split the responses between teens and others (parents, teachers and coaches). There are some great ideas here and, as we move forward with the Better Human movement, we hope to help teens branch out and start initiatives within their local or global communities. With social media as a backdrop, reaching out has never been easier.

Comments from Teenagers

Positive and wholesome community.

They would volunteer in local activities and events, along with helping build a sense of community amongst neighbors.

To make a better community, teenagers should volunteer in the community, such as help elders who cannot shoveling their sidewalk.

Participating in community events and volunteering their time.

These teenagers are going to turn into Adults pretty soon, so they would be positive, contributing members to their communities. Whether this is through community events or just the overall upkeep/safety in the community.

Help bring the community together, help eliminate stressors different groups feel within the community. Support each other.

Standing up for what is right, standing firm in their beliefs, displaying courage and leading others in building a community of trust.

Helping out others whenever possible, volunteering, making donations, coordinating community events.

Positive roles within the community create well being of people within the community at large.

The community would notice the actions of the teenager and start applying those into their lives. They will understand the impact that the teenager has on their lives.

They'd help out by volunteering or be respectful to public and/or private property. They'd be respectful of people and the rules.

Organize fundraisers, events, etc for causes bigger than themselves. Create safe places for those who need it. Offer to help those who need it, such as seniors, etc (lawn care, snow removal, groceries, dog walking).

Recognize the unseen, unnoticed or neglected groups such as homeless, senior citizens, economically challenged.

Create stronger communities, better relationships.

Community environment would become more positive and they will be more open to accepting different types of people.

It would encourage other teenagers to help out as well.

Actively engaged in making the community a better place for all.

Change community perceptions of teenagers. Allow those isolated to still feel part of the community by helping the elderly and those who are unable to help themselves. Positive actions are addicting.

Comments from Parents, Teachers & Coaches

I think they would show their community how to become better people and how to help each other in more ways than one. They would have a positive spread throughout their community that would help people become more selfless and open to other causes or problems besides their own.

People among communities will be more interactive with one another, hence more ongoing peaceful events with lots of participation.

They would start doing the things everyone talks about but haven't gotten around to.

They would try to aid their community whether it be through chores for neighbours or volunteer service.

They could make an impact and make others feel welcomed and loved in their community.

A Better Human Teenager would volunteer in their community, whether it be in a senior home, cleaning up the community, or helping run a community event.

Being more engaged.

Strong relationships with neighbors, volunteer, friendliness.

Positive, be involved. Attend community events or better yet fund raise for them. Help thy neighbours.

BHT's presence in the community can help to shift the preconceived notions of how a teenager behaves and what they can offer.

What impact would a Better Human Teenager have on their home?

When we asked, "What impact would a Better Human Teenager have on their home?", we heard both suggestions for how teens can positively impact their home, as well as descriptions of what that home could be and feel like, which we suppose are intertwined. But it's interesting to see how many people jumped to offering suggestions rather than imagine the impact of those suggestions.

Those who focused on suggestions said things like contribute to the household, be an involved family member, lead by example and act as a role model for younger siblings, show respect for parents - dare we assume most of these suggestions come from overwhelmed parents?

Comments that focused on how a home is *impacted* as a result of teens who show up as "Better," which was the intent of the question, offered things like fewer fights between family members, less angst, more harmony, love and laughter, a place to feel safe and loved no matter what, a sense of family and togetherness, better communication, stronger relationships, interdependence, a healthy and optimistic environment. One parent offered "I believe that an amiable and thoughtful teenager can transform the overall feeling in the home and subconsciously encourages positive interactions between mom and dad as well as siblings." It's really quite amazing to hear that a positive, respectful, helpful teen can have this kind of incredible impact on their home and family.

There were a few responses about how teens can educate their parents on new social and political issues and about bridging gaps. Intriguing! It's not something we as authors and researchers had assumed we would hear. But we love it! Our teens are young *and* they have brilliant minds, fresh perspectives, and their fingers on the pulse of current issues. Why shouldn't we be learning from them? These comments came from teenage respondents themselves. Maybe adults should sit up and listen.

One comment in particular really strikes a chord and is a powerful highlight from the survey: "It's not being perfect all the time, but it's doing the best you can that day, that moment." How profound to allow for imperfection and simply trying to be our best in each moment.

Comments From Teenagers

Families will have less arguments that are based on disagreement, because they will have better communication with each family member. Disputes will be settled in a peaceful, reasonable manner.

They would have stronger relationships and value interdependence.

Strengthening their relationships and being able to bring a sense of family and togetherness at home.

A Better Human Teenager would help contribute to the welfare of their household. For example, they would take initiative with household chores or act independently and responsibly, to not burden their household members.

They would try to understand the different perspectives within their home, and try to extend the same love and kindness towards family, even if they're at odds with one another.

Understanding and grateful of parents' efforts, educating parents on new social and political issues.

Supporting the family choices, developing his/her family to stay connected together.

They would assist in bringing a sense of life and joy within the household and to take part in activities with the rest of family.

Helping out in the household, learning to not only care for themselves, but others in their family.

Unify and strengthen family ties, be someone their parents can be proud of, willingly take up family responsibilities such as chores.

They would make their home a better living environment with positive energy. They would do this by respecting their parents as well as their siblings to help make a positive impact within the household.

They would help out and start conversations with family, creating a more open environment.

The teenager and others living within the home would be in a bright and positive mood. They will have an honest, loving, and open relationship with each other.

At home, they treat their family the way they want to be treated. Even during arguments, they find a way to put their anger away and solve the problem. They educate their *family about ongoing issues in the community and society, while encouraging them to help out and volunteer! They also practice affection and improve on their communication skills.*

A good impact, especially right now when we are all home together more than we usually are. I think that people could put a greater amount of focus into making our own homes a better place.

Spreading joy and laughter and inspiring family bonding.

Understanding and patience. Knowing that they can't change other people or their responses to things. Simply being there to support the people around them. It's not being perfect all the time, but it's doing the best you can that day; that moment.

Comments from Parents, Teachers & Coaches

Ability to promote change and improvement across multiple generations.

Participate in the family and also participate in family chores.

Kindness begets kindness! I believe that an amiable and thoughtful teenager can transform the overall feeling in the home and subconsciously encourages positive interactions between mom and dad as well as siblings.

More communication with parents will equal less resistance, more understanding, and more trust.

Oh my gosh, don't get me started! A teenager who thinks broader than themselves would do a 180 for the home! Offer

Margins, help around the house, build morale, let family members know they're appreciated and loved.

Contributing to the household. Appreciating the importance of family.

That's a tough one. Even the best kid still thinks their parents suck ass sometimes. However, they are open, engaged and involved.

Less angst. More harmony. More love and laughter.

This is the place where they can be vulnerable and open about the good, the bad and all the stuff in between. A place to feel safe, loved, no matter what.

They spend a lot of time at school but if things at home aren't right, it's tough for them to be Better Human beings here. This is a tricky one because they need positive influences at home in order to be Better Human teenagers.

Stronger relationships, better communication.

Peace... working at understanding others.

What impact would a Better Human Teenager have on the world?

We heard very impassioned responses to our question "What impact would a Better Human Teenager have on the world?" Young people are the future. No one can dispute that. Whether they become the world's next leaders, scientists, teachers, parents, they will make choices, decisions and changes that impact where our world heads. According to our survey responses, parents, teachers, and teens alike feel they are a generation looking at some of the world's most difficult problems and it would serve us well to sit up and listen to what they have to say. They envision a world that encourages young people to voice their perspectives, especially when they differ from those of adults; a world where everyone feels accepted and can express themselves.

This generation sees themselves as visionaries with goals and passions who can have an incredibly positive impact on the world and they are prepared to work hard to do it. One respondent offered that teens need to give their voice to matters that are important to them and to ensure their voices are not forgotten or neglected by past generations currently in charge. Wow. They are prepared to speak up for what they believe is right. Can you say the same about you?

Many responses called out activism for environmental and social justice matters, like inequality and poverty, as particularly important issues they want to address. Many comments centered on advocating for human welfare, especially for those who don't have the opportunity to advocate for themselves, to help fight for the rights of others and not just for those that resemble them.

And finally, peace was offered as a resulting impact on the world of teens being "Better." Peace. What an incredible vision.

Comments from Teenagers

Tear down stereotypes, promote equality, solve humanity's most complex problems, improve quality of life for others.

The agent for change, a Better Human Teenager would show individuals around the world that it's okay to not be okay, that it's okay to be different, we all bleed the same colour. We are all human. A Better Human Teenager would take action in standing up for not only their own beliefs, but learn to show courage to others, so that they may also find confidence within themselves.

A Better Human Teenager can change the world if they put their mind to it. If they are devoted to what they're trying to achieve, sooner or later the world will start to recognize them and support them.

Teenagers will be more active in worldwide issues, giving their perspectives on things that may not be brought up by adults. Different people in different stages of life have different experiences, so they all have valuable perspectives that should be taken into consideration in order for the world to head towards a brighter future.

They would be someone that others can come to for any kind of support. It could be to cheer others up, to be a good friend, or to generally be kind. They should inspire others to try new things and give them motivation towards goals they'd like to achieve.

They would have a clear vision and goal of how they want to change the world!

A Better Human Teenager would impact the world in a positive way. They could slowly make it a better place where everyone feels accepted.

Become the next leaders or other extremely important positions (scientists, teachers) to make changes for the next generations. They have to be passionate.

They would make it safer and a place where you can express yourself.

They would advocate for those who don't have the opportunity to advocate for themselves, and they would understand that a small change can lead to a huge effect.

A Better Human Teenager would be kind wherever they go, help people out wherever they go, be generous, and from a digital perspective, not post anything rude or unkind.

The agent for change, a Better Human Teenager would show individuals around the world that it's okay to not be okay, that it's okay to be different, we all bleed the same colour. We are all human. A Better Human Teenager would take action in standing up for not only their own beliefs, but learn to show courage to others, so that they may also find confidence within themselves.

I envision the Better Human Teenager would feel a sense of responsibility to better the world. They would be an activist for environmental and social justice issues. The amount of impact their actions have would be equal to the impact potential, as world issues would be very important to this person.

They would help us realize there is still humanity left in people and that people care about the world. Other people would start to realize their actions and start applying those into their lives to help make the world a better living place.

The Better Human Teenager would have a positive and significant impact on the world. It could be something as small as a volunteerism group, to something as big as a systematic change. They are recognized for the work they do, but do not seek any reward for their work. What they do is purely of heart and only to help those in need. They see a problem in society and address it in whatever way possible. Small actions lead to big change.

They would use their voice and actions to create a meaningful change that would inspire other teenagers from around the world to follow suit.

Better Human Teenagers are visionaries. They have goals and passions that they work towards, and they are always utilizing more of their potential.

Comments from Parents, Teachers & Coaches

Not afraid to tackle anything! Elevation of the human experience.

Creating understanding.

Tear down stereotypes, promote equality, solve humanity's most complex problems, improve quality of life for others.

Less fighting or bullying.

They could start movements.

Lead by example and encourage others to do the same is one step toward influencing the world. The "ripple effect."

Would be informed on world issues and contribute to change.

I feel that if they believe in the greater good, they can make a big impact. I think this generation has a ton of information at their fingertips to make the world a much better place.

They represent a new generation looking at some of the world's most difficult problems. I think they have fresh eyes, ideas and technology that they could apply to these problems.

This is a HUGE one - more awareness about how to fix the world in terms of the environment, better and hopefully more honest politics. They are our future, so the decisions they make really set the tone for where our world heads.

What things could teenagers do to be Better Humans?

What is something you have done, or want to do, that makes you feel like a Better Human?

In our survey, we asked the questions: "What things could teenagers do to be Better Humans?" and "What is something you have done, or want to do, that makes you feel like a Better Human?" What was so interesting was that the different groups of respondents had diverse perspectives in many ways, but they shared similar perspectives in others. We designed the survey respondents to identify themselves in the following groups:

 – Parent
 – Teenager
 – Teacher or coach of teenagers
 – Not a parent but know some great teenagers

The consistent and unwavering message from all groups was the act of helping others is the key to achieving Better Human status. Things like working at a food bank or soup kitchen, tutoring and mentoring younger kids, participating in shoreline cleanups, volunteering at school, taking care of neighbours, helping kids with disabilities, and taking care of the elderly were common examples offered by all respondents.

Is this the secret to being a Better Human? As you read the interviews later in this book, pause to see how each of the teens is making a true difference. Where is their focus? Is it in their bedrooms playing video games or hanging out at the mall? The answer seems obvious when you read their stories.

It would have been interesting to ask why that outward focus is so important. Does it change their perspective? Does it make them feel alive? Does it really make a difference to them and those they are helping? What is the degree of difference it makes to help another person?

What you'll also notice through reading these real comments from survey respondents is that the volunteering didn't always include acts that were significant by any means; many of them were really very simple.

Comments from Teenagers

I have previously helped a little boy who fell and injured his knees. I piggy backed him to a bench and helped him with his injuries with my first aid kit that I carry around. I then called his parents to come pick him up.

I have helped the elderly cross the street many times.

I've helped strangers in public do things that aren't difficult for me but are difficult for them. This ranged from helping a woman who missed her bus call a taxi, and letting kids in the library use the computer I was using cause they needed it more. All it cost me was a few minutes of my time.

Be more respectful of others, help more with no reward.

Pick up garbage.

Drop something off for someone who is going through a hard time - a letter, a note, a kind word.

Put down their phones.

Spending more time connecting with real people.

To simply be kind to one another.

Comments from Parents, Teachers & Coaches

Take time away from their screens to show random acts of kindness each day.

Be respectful and help neighbours by doing small things to help them out, even if they were to just bring in their garbage cans.

Learn that they can make a difference one positive connection at a time. Set a personal goal to make one positive connection every day.

When we asked the question: *"What things could teenagers do to be Better Humans?"* it was somewhat surprising to hear how the same message was relayed from both the adult and teenager perspective. The message put forth was clearly focused on the development of the person as an individual as opposed to the human act of always doing something for others. There were so many recommendations on exactly what was important, and it was surprising to see so many teens focusing on the development of their *character*. These following comments from parents really jumped out at us:

Teens need to start thinking of more than themselves and start thinking of gratitude and purpose.

Thoughtful, considerate kind humans caring about more than themselves. Being selfless.

Stop being self-absorbed, stop focusing on video games, put down their phones, pick up anything else, a shovel to dig, a ball to play, a mouth to speak, a book to read.

Be accountable. Respect consequences for your actions. Live within your means. Educate themselves on how to deal with their physical and mental fitness. What can they do to make meaningful changes in their lives? As parents we have a tendency to handle our kid's problems for them rather than guide them through handling those problems themselves. Our kids can handle more than we think. Let's focus on filling their tool boxes with tools that will serve them later in life.

Be open to multiple, competing perspectives in search for shared truths. Commit to learning, instead of knowing... take time to listen. Take time to share learnings with others. Volunteer.

Notice what's going on around them and in the world." This includes advice on becoming more aware of other people's perspectives, and cultures. Speak up for social and political issues, learn more about the world around us, speak up when something's wrong, listen to others' opinions and values to further develop our own.

I want to stop procrastinating on the things that matter to me. I want to start working now to make the person I dream about being someday.

We wondered if the teens who answered this question held part of the secret once again to being a Better Human. Did they possess a higher level of understanding; of enlightenment? The overarching theme was clearly on the development of their mindset based on these answers. What do you think?

The act of being selfless is more than being a better human. It's showing others how to be the best human one could be.

Think of others, have hope, act with optimism and have hope for the future.

Be kind, and learn to listen before casting judgement. Volunteer more, and stand up for other people.

Stop comparing yourself to others to make yourself feel better, speak up for people you see being bullied, speak up for social and political issues, be kind and empathetic to the people around you.

Work on themselves to make themselves a better person before trying to change others!

Find a support system, people you can be yourself around, people who will support you in everything you do. Learn to understand, to look at things from another perspective before opening your mouth and shutting others out.

Trying to be more self-aware, and to try to stop following the crowd. In this way, more ideas and innovations will be developed and created, to better our world, communities, and relationships.

We wonder what jumps out for you as a teen from the survey questions above. What resonates? What's your big takeaway from this survey data? What else would you add, and what do you think should have been included? We'd love to hear from you! Send us an email at bebetter@betterhumangroup.com and let us know.

Interview Methodology

If you've ever been interviewed, you know that the experience can be pressure filled and off putting. Put on the spot to answer thought provoking questions can cause people to freeze and unable to express how they truly feel and think. Adding to the complexity of these particular interviews was the fact that we were talking with teens and wanted to ensure we had their parents' support for our project and how we were proposing to involve their kids.

We took a multi-stage approach to combat these challenges.

First, in most cases, we reached out to the teen's parents and provided an explanation of what we were up to, what we were hoping to accomplish, and how we wanted to involve their teen. Then we talked to the teens themselves, explaining the same thing. It was important to us that everyone involved was comfortable and supportive of our mission.

Next, to allow the interviewee some "soak time" with our questions, we emailed them a simple document and asked them to type out their initial reactions and responses. When these responses were sent back to us, we read through them and noted our reactions and additional questions we intended to ask. It was during follow up conversations that we were able to dig deeper to uncover what the teen wanted to convey; to help them tell their story.

Interestingly, many of the teens had never thought of themselves as "Better Humans," or exceptional in any way. They all had a true humbleness about themselves. Giving them time to privately think about who they are and why they do what they do, then asking for more details, allowed us to uncover the real them.

Our ultimate goal was to help tell the stories of these exceptional young people in hopes that would encourage others to step up and take action. We think our approach has resulted in just that.

Interview Insights

By design, our interviews allowed us to really dig into why Better Human Teenagers do what they do. In asking questions about what drives them, many gained self-awareness about who they are at their core. Our transcripts of the interviews are gold mines of inspirational quotes and the chills we interviewers felt while talking to these awesome young people were endless.

We wanted to understand what makes these Better Human Teenagers tick. What is it that lives inside of them that drives them to do caring and compassionate things? What or who inspires them to do what they do? Are they a certain type of person? Do they all come from parents who are also "Better?" Have they all had similar upbringings? Do they come from similar backgrounds or circumstances? Do they need to be a certain age to really have impact?

What we learned is that each individual has his or her own story; their own reason for behaving as they do; their own catalyst for what first sparked their desire to be better. They have different backgrounds, histories, experiences, and family make ups. Their ages range. Some did really big things and some made small kind and caring acts part of their every day. Some have teams of cheer leaders behind them, some have fewer. Some experienced pushback, distrust and bullying because of their kind acts. There aren't strong similarities among this impressive group. But what they all have is empathy for others, courage, and they have heart.

We also learned that many of the teens are involved in organized extracurricular activities; for many it was sports. We don't believe it is the act of competing in sport that is the secret ingredient; it's the commitment, dedication and hard work required by sport that teaches an individual to apply these same things to how they live their life.

Something else we heard multiple times was that young people have the luxury of time and don't have the bigger burdens of responsibility that come with being an adult, but they sometimes lack the courage, the ideas, or the opportunities to get involved in Better Human work. Maybe if we create more opportunities for young people to get involved, and make it easy and accessible for them to do so, more of them will take us up on the offer! Let's help make it easy.

The next 140 or so pages contain the transcripts of 21 interviews with some phenomenal teenagers doing their part to make this world a better place. It is our hope that you feel chills like we did, that you see yourself in some of the stories, that you feel inspired to find what you really care about, and that you are encouraged to take action; to make an impact on this world, in any way that feels right for you.

Stories compiled by Steve Brierley

50 Burgers and a Bandana

An interview with Perry Brierley - Now 21 years old, in university, working towards a business degree, but 17 years old when this story happened.

What does it mean to be a Better Human?

For me the idea of being a Better Human is to always try to help other people that have less than you or simply need some help. It's about looking around you and when you see someone needs a hand, give them a hand. It's really simple but it does take work and constantly being aware of what is going on in your life.

Why is it important to be a Better Human?

I really think it's important to give back to other people. The more we give back, the better our community and society will be. Giving back helps to define our community and society.

Tell me a story about a time when you did something to be a Better Human. What was the impact? How did it make you feel? Did you have any challenges?

I was hanging out with two friends, Jeric and Eugene, and we were feeling very fortunate about our lives. We enjoyed school, had good friends, a supportive family, a place to sleep, food to eat, had part-time jobs and we had some money in our pockets to buy things that we wanted. As we started to talk about the people around us, we realized there are so many people who do not have the same things we had. It was especially noticeable when we walked around downtown and saw all the homeless people begging for money to buy food. We honestly started to feel a little guilty and tried to think of ways that we could help.

As we discussed the problem, the conversation turned to what made us feel better and we immediately thought of food and how some things felt like a treat. It was at that time we came to a simple conclusion, BURGERS! Whenever we wanted to treat ourselves it meant a trip to McDonald's to grab a burger and fries. The natural conclusion we came to was, "Let's buy some homeless people burgers to help brighten up their day." If it worked for us it would most likely work for them.

So we gathered our money and went to a local McD's to order single burgers. The total cost was less than $75 so we split the cost and bought the 50 burgers. It was quite exciting to order the burgers and we were very excited to see how it went although we were a little nervous about how the burgers would be accepted.

With our bag of burgers in hand, we went to an area where the local homeless people hung out and we approached our first person. We were honestly quite nervous, as in our daily life we would never really have a conversation with homeless people. The unfortunate truth is they were mostly invisible to us. It was time to change that. The first person we approached was certainly confused with our offering but gladly accepted the burger and said thanks. Surprisingly, it felt great to give the first burger away. It made us want to work quicker and give all the burgers away as soon as possible.

Two things happened that surprised us and helped us learn some great lessons about people. Some people simply refused the burger with a comment like "I am ok" or "I don't need anything." It was a shocking response as we thought everyone would want a burger. It really spoke to us how not everyone has the same values when it comes to getting food for free. The lesson learned was that maybe we should have asked people what they want instead of imposing our own values on them.

The second lesson had the greatest impact. We approached a guy and offered him a burger. He said he would accept on one condition; we had to take something from him. Here was a guy living on the streets with very little and he wanted to give us something. He had pride and wanted us to understand that no matter what your situation, you can help others. He reached into his pocket and pulled out a bandana. He then said the burger for the bandana would be a fair trade. Reluctantly, we agreed. The second lesson learned was powerful. Human spirit and pride do not always leave when you are down on your luck! This exchange gave us an extra spring in our step and we quickly gave away all the burgers. It was such an incredible day I will never forget!

What is something specific you want to do to be a Better Human?

The most important thing is really simple, just help others any way you can. It doesn't need to be some grand plan but just do something you feel comfortable doing. Spend less time thinking and more time doing.

What advice would you give to teens if they want to be Better Humans today?

Don't try to change the world, just try to help change one person. Changing the world is such a daunting task but doing something simple for someone is easy and takes very little effort.

Is there something/someone that inspires you to be a Better Human?

My mom has always inspired me with how she always gives money to people on the street. She will go out of her way to meet homeless people and try to help. It's the spirit my mom has towards giving back that inspired me to give away the burgers.

Also, inspiration is all around us all the time. If you are connected at all to any social media you can read about and see pictures of people being Better Humans all the time. The trick is to simply step back and let the stories in social media sink in and then do something about it.

Has your life changed as a result of being a Better Human? Tell me how.

The biggest thing is that I know I have to give back to people who have less than me. If I want the world to be a better place then we need to have Better Humans. Just give back!

Tell me why young people can make a difference in the world if they take action.

Young people are full of ideas and energy. It's time to take that energy and focus on how we can help other people around us, regardless of what's going on in our life. I really think we probably felt better giving the burgers away than the people did receiving the burgers. If you want to feel good, do good!

Steve's Reflections

I heard about this story while my wife Alex and I were sitting around talking with Perry about volunteering. It was great for me to hear this story as I wasn't aware of this when it happened. (Full disclosure this is my son) I found two things quite interesting about this story. One, not everyone wanted a burger. I guess it's important to try and connect with others and find out exactly how we can help. The second point was how some felt a need to give back even though they had little to give. What a strong message about the human spirit! Overall, it was inspiring for me to hear about three kids getting together with a plan and a good heart to help others. I know it would have been tough to approach people on the street to offer something so I admire the approach they chose to give back. I found this story very inspiring and have started to do something similar.

Little Things Make a Big Difference

An interview with Reed, a 17 year old volunteer extraordinaire at school, home, and in the community. Big outdoor person who loves to get into the woods.

What does it mean to be a Better Human?

Being a Better Human means being selfless, giving back to others who may not have what you have. Ideally, you do this everyday but sometimes it's important to do a little bit extra. Also, initially it is sometimes difficult to give back but at the end of the day, it always feels great to help others. It also means being a great brother and son. Family is important.

Why is it important to be a Better Human?

When we help others, the impact can be felt by many other people, not just the person you are helping. For example, when I volunteer at school I know that everyone that goes to the school will be impacted because when students give back and help out, the culture of the school is impacted.

I believe trying to be a Better Human is different for everyone. For someone else, it may mean just being nice to people around you to create a good environment, where for me it means doing something very specific where the person feels a direct impact. I think the more people that try to be Better Humans, the better our world can be. The key word is selflessness.

Also, when you give back, you can make the community better. Giving back can have a "chain reaction effect" because if you impact and inspire someone, that can help them do the same thing, and so on. Ultimately you could start helping one person and then others could become involved.

Tell me a story about a time when you did something to be a Better Human. What was the impact? How did it make you feel? Did you have any challenges?

The setting for the first story is in my hometown and on my block. Unfortunately, it also involves something that most people have a love/hate relationship with, snow. My grandparents spend time every year living just a few houses down from our house so we can be close to them. As frequent travellers, they spend a lot of time abroad but when they are here, our family focus is to make sure they are comfortable. With the frequent snow storms we have, I do spend a good amount of time shovelling around our house but when my grandparents are nearby, the volume of shovelling goes up dramatically.

As a practice, whenever we have a snow storm, I walk down to their house and shovel their steps and driveway. Since I already have a shovel in hand, I usually shovel all the walks along the way which is about 10 homes. It really doesn't take me long and when I'm finished, I feel great about being able to do this physical work. Most people really don't like shovelling so I know they appreciate it when I actually clean their walks. It's also a great workout for me!

The second part of my story is helping kids get back into the woods. I personally find that when I get into the woods, it changes your mind about life and helps you reconnect. This year I was supposed to take a camp counsellor course but because of Covid-19, camp was cancelled, which was very disappointing. Ultimately my goal is to spend time helping kids get into the woods during all seasons of the year. Personally, I did an 18 day backcountry trip recently and I plan to help other kids get the same experience I got when I did the trip.

What is something specific you want to do to be a Better Human?

My long term plan is to become an Environmental Engineer so I can help make the world a better place. I really believe that if we don't take care of the planet, we will not have great lives.

What advice would you give to teens if they want to be Better Humans today?

You don't have to do big things to make a big difference. I think it's easy to get paralyzed into not giving back because there are so many things we can do to help each other. Therefore, just pick something small, and do it. Then pick something else, and do it. It doesn't need to be complicated and it doesn't have to involve large groups of people. Just find something you like to do, like even helping kids with homework, and make it happen.

When you think about doing something to give back or help others, just take little steps and before you know, you will have done some great things to help others.

Is there something/someone that inspires you to be a Better Human?

My parents are very inspirational to me. They both are always looking for ways to give back and I was raised to give back. I would say our family focuses on giving back and that has rubbed off on me.

Also, going to camp has been very inspirational. At camp I am surrounded by great people who focus on simply being nice to others. When you combine that with being in the woods, camp is such a great place to really become a person that helps others.

Has your life changed as a result of being a Better Human? Tell me how.

One thing about giving back is it just makes you feel good to help others. I notice that when I do something nice for someone, the feeling is great. What's interesting is when you are being nice to others, it feels good to you. It makes you want to give back so you can feel great. That is the power of selflessness.

Tell me why young people can make a difference in the world if they take action.

One main reason is that every generation learns from the previous generation, so as a group of highly energetic people, we can take the information and do things to change the world, make it a better place. The most important thing is to remember we are learning lessons of what not to do and what to do.

Steve's Reflections

Meeting Reed helped me to get a better understanding of how small steps into volunteering can have a huge impact. The key word for me out of this interview is "selfless." This word comes up in all my interviews but it was front and centre with Reed. He is very clear about how volunteering impacts him and based on his future plans, I think he will live a life of giving back. When you combine his passion for the outdoors, his education and volunteerism, Reed will be a positive force in this world.

A Beautiful Renovation

An interview with Riley Hopper, 18 yr old hockey player, volunteer extraordinaire and all around good guy who gives back to others. He calls himself "Uber" for all the times he picks up friends and drives them around!

What does it mean to be a Better Human?

A Better Human is someone who thinks about others before they think about themselves. It's a person who will go out of their way and be uncomfortable doing things to help other people, regardless of the situation. A Better Human is selfless and thinks about the world but, in my case, focuses on the people near me.

Why is it important to be a Better Human?

When you are a Better Human, you make people feel good by doing things for them. You can have a direct impact on how their days go and what their life can be like. The other thing that's important is if you give back, maybe that person will also give back and you can create a wave of people giving back. If that happens, the world just becomes a better place to live for everyone.

Tell me a story about a time when you did something to be a Better Human. What was the impact? How did it make you feel? Did you have any challenges?

Earlier this year, just around the time Covid-19 hit, my mom shared a story about a local business, Pin-Ups Hair Shoppe in Bowness, that needed to be renovated and updated but with the business closed, the owner was in a tough position with no cash flow. The shop was in desperate need for a facelift but no money to do the work. Also, the owner's husband had just died of cancer and as a single mom of two kids, life was challenging.

So my mom Angela met with me at the kitchen table and asked if I wanted to change someone's life. As a person who is constantly doing volunteer work around the city, I jumped at the opportunity. Together we created a devious plan to fix the hair shop while the owner was away looking after family members. Pin Ups is such a strong local business. The shop provides regular hair services to the neighbourhood and most importantly for me, the owner dyed all the player's hair blonde on my hockey team at no charge for a fundraiser we were doing. I knew I had to give back. The plan was simple. As soon as the owner went away, we would tear down the interior and rebuild to give it a fresh new look. We spoke to the landlord and the plan started.

We tore down the interior and started to rebuild. I didn't really know how to do the work but I learned on the job. I learned new skills like how to put down tile and basic carpentry. Once we started working, things just seemed to flow and after 6 weeks of doing 4 to 14-hour days, the shop had been completely renovated. Something really cool happened along the way. As I started telling people about the renovation plan, they wanted to help. In a short time, the entire hockey team was helping, other friends of the family were donating products for the renovation and it was an amazing feeling to be part of this.

The day of the reveal was filled with emotions. As you can imagine, the owner burst into tears when she saw the shop for the first time and there wasn't a dry eye in the shop. The last 6 weeks had been tough but it felt great to see the finished work.

What is something specific you want to do to be a Better Human?

With all the experience I have volunteering, I want to make sure that whatever career I choose I always have time to volunteer and give back. It's very important to me to help others. Maybe I can even think about working in a job where I help other people professionally. That would be ideal.

What advice would you give to teens if they want to be Better Humans today?

Just start volunteering. Do anything. Don't overthink this. The amazing thing is when you volunteer, it draws others to do the same. I think teens are afraid to start things maybe because they're shy but once you decide to volunteer, you will meet some amazing people.

Is there something/someone that inspires you to be a Better Human?

My parents, Angela and Mark, have inspired me to be a Better Human by being good role models. They are always thinking and doing things for other people which has truly inspired me to do the same. The cool thing is when I volunteer, I probably feel better than the person that is receiving the volunteer work. It's such a great feeling to help others even when you are going through tough times. I hope I also inspire others with all the volunteer work I do.

Has your life changed as a result of being a Better Human? Tell me how.

The biggest change is how I think about and see the world. I know I can give back and I'm constantly looking for ways to volunteer. The selfless act of volunteering has a way of coming back and making you feel great about yourself.

Tell me why young people can make a difference in the world if they take action.

We are full of energy and just need some direction on what to do. When we work together to help others, there is no stopping us! We are a force to be reckoned with. We just need to take the first step!

Steve's Reflections

I met Riley through his mom, Angela. I interviewed Riley while he was working one of his many jobs. Besides all the sports (name one and he plays it), part-time work and volunteer work, he made time to meet me so he could share his story. Riley has the gift of spreading energy and enthusiasm in his actions. It was the drive that brought his hockey teammates to join him in the renovation. The power of inspiration is something we need more of and with his focus on helping others, he has the opportunity to create a movement of teen volunteers when he gets a chance to tell his story so please, SHARE HIS STORY!

You've got the Power to be a Better Human!

An interview with Emily Frezell, passionate about people, personal health, and bumper plates!

What does it mean to be a Better Human?

Being a Better Human is all about helping other people. It's taking the skills you have and sharing those skills with others. Helping people get better, whatever that means for that person. I think we all have skills that others would love to learn, so sharing them is just a simple way of helping. The more we can help others, the better people can be, which will end up making our schools, communities, and the world a better place.

Why is it important to be a Better Human?

When we help others, they get better. When they get better, so does their life. When their life gets better, so does everything around them. Better life, better world!

Tell me a story about a time when you did something to be a Better Human. What was the impact? How did it make you feel? Did you have any challenges?

My story started in grade 10 when I was having some issues with stress and I needed a way to get rid of frustrations in a healthy way. My family is very focused on fitness and with the introduction to fitness from my dad, I started lifting weights as a way to get rid of some extra energy.

As soon as I started lifting, I realized I found something that I loved and something that I was good at. With extra encouragement from my friend Zack, I really started to look forward to every workout and lifting weights turned into powerlifting. For those who don't know what that is, it's lifting your maximum weight for squat, deadlift and bench press. It's a very hardcore sport and requires discipline, dedication and strong mental capability to push through pain and do something you think you can't do, like lift double or more of your body weight.

I quickly realized that doing this type of workout was having a deep impact on how I felt about myself. It helped me to overcome the fear of people judging me and I no longer really cared about what other people thought of me. It allowed me to just be a teenager and spend more time enjoying life. That's when I realized I could help other people feel the way I feel. So, I started an Instagram page to share my story and began to post pics and videos of my workouts. I did this because I have always just wanted to help other people.

It started at a young age for me, to help others, as I grew up in an environment where helping others is just what you should do. I think showing the workouts started to inspire others to exercise, as I soon had over 3000 followers, which I still can't believe. Besides the workouts, I also started to post information on nutrition and how to live a healthy lifestyle. It was a great feeling to know that so many people were being inspired by my story. What felt especially great was when I found out I helped two friends change their lifestyle and embrace health.

Sharing my workout information and seeing people get inspired has made me feel very accomplished and proud. Because of this success, I plan to continue my fitness journey and become a personal trainer. My future goal is to go to SAIT and become certified for fitness and maybe become a firefighter. My dream is to inspire thousands of people to live a healthy lifestyle and realize as long as you put your mind into it, you can do anything you want and inspire others along the way.

What is something specific you want to do to be a Better Human?

I want to live a life of service and give back to others. I plan to do it with my fitness workouts but also in my career. I hope to become a firefighter but whatever I end up doing, it will be to help others.

What advice would you give to teens if they want to be Better Humans today?

Start giving back and you will make others feel great and you will feel great. Don't worry about what others will think or about being judged. Just go out and help others and you will be surprised just how good it feels.

Is there something/someone that inspires you to be a Better Human?

I have two role models for fitness that inspire me. One is a bodybuilder named Steve Cook. His knowledge and workouts help me to keep going to the gym. He is a two-time Mr. Olympia champion and has over 1.3 million followers on YouTube (my workout inspiration). The other person I am truly inspired by is The Rock, Dwayne Johnson. He has such a positive attitude, gives back to people and is just a nice human being. My dream is to one day meet him in person.

Has your life changed as a result of being a Better Human? Tell me how.

Giving back to others has had such a great impact on my life. I am more confident, and most importantly, knowing how important it is to give back, I make it something I do everyday.

Tell me why young people can make a difference in the world if they take action.

As teens, we don't know how much impact we have because we mostly hear bad stories about us. We can change that and become a force that changes the world. The most important thing to remember is we all can do something to make a difference in other people's lives. Wash your neighbor's car, shovel their driveway, smile at the store clerk, ask a homeless person their name and have a quick chat. Just do something for other people and you will see the difference it can make.

Steve's Reflections

I met Emily through her dad, Mark Frezell. This is a story of perseverance, resilience and success. Not mentioned in the interview is that Emily was preparing for her first ever powerlifting competition in March but unfortunately, due to Covid-19, it was cancelled. Emily's story is one where, regardless of the situation, she moved forward and never let obstacles get in her way. Not only that, she used her experience to help others in a most positive way. Emily's dedication and discipline has made her a force to be reckoned with and I bet she will achieve any goals she sets for herself in life! A true role model!

All Smiles For a Hot Pink Dress

An interview with Izzy Bradley, 19, with boundless energy on the volleyball court, organizing events, leading a charity drive and helping other people to feel welcome.

What does it mean to be a better human?

Life is about caring for others, giving back and being selfless, not selfish (concerned more with the needs and wishes of others than with one's own). It's really important to give back even if it hurts a little. The more we give back, the better the world will be.

Why is it important to be a better human?

It's important because when we give back, it makes the world a better place. The biggest impact is that it creates happiness for other people and makes their lives better. It's really not complicated but it is so important.

Tell me a story about a time when you did something to be a Better Human. What was the impact? How did it make you feel? Did you have any challenges?

My story is about working as a volunteer for My Best Friend's Closet, part of the Making Changes Association (www.

makingchangesassociation.ca). The organization helps young women between the ages of 12-18 by providing gently used clothing. As part of my volunteer work, I start off by creating a clothing drive asking friends through school, volleyball, and my community to donate clothes. Everyone of my friends has at least a few clothing items they have hardly worn and can give away. I gathered hundreds of really great items to donate to My Best Friends Closet. As a volunteer, I help clients decide what they want to give away and bring the clothes to the Making Changes store.

My best day ever was when one particular young woman came into the store. She was new to Canada and very shy. My job as a Peer Stylist, is to make all the girls feel welcome and help build a wardrobe of clothes she would love to have. I started doing this volunteer work when I was 16 years old. Like most of the girls that come and shop, this girl was reluctant to take anything for free, but you could tell she was excited to be there.

After some time talking, laughing and connecting, she finally opened up and said her favorite colour was hot pink. Well that started the whole process of shopping. After a search through all the great clothes, we found a hot pink dress. Her eyes lit up! With the find, she went into the change room and tried on the new dress. When she came out she was ecstatic. I have never seen such a huge smile on someone before!! You could see her self-esteem grow instantly. The dress was a big hit and we continued to shop for the rest of the afternoon, finding items that she could take with her. It was at that moment I understood the power of helping others. I spent the rest of the day helping other girls get clothes and that sense of helping had such a tremendous impact on me.

There are some challenges as a Peer Stylist, as most of the girls are shy, some have language challenges with English, and most importantly, they do not always feel comfortable in the store setting. That's where my school sports experience and love of leadership help me to connect with each of the girls and build up some trust. Working with and getting new clothes is exciting no matter what your background!

What is something specific you want to do to be a Better Human?

My goal is to become a teacher, certainly with a language focus, and ultimately join Teachers Without Borders. I would love to travel the world and teach people French or English. I believe the better we can communicate, the better the world will be. I really want to help people that are less fortunate, and I think being able to teach a language will be very helpful everywhere.

What advice would you give to teens if they want to be Better Humans today?

If you want to help others, you just need to make the time. No excuses, just get it done. If you don't make it a priority you probably won't do it. I think the thing people need to realize is you need to make sacrifices in life to help others but if you do, you will love how you feel. Find something you are passionate about and turn that into volunteer work.

Is there something/someone that inspires you to be a Better Human?

My mom is my greatest inspiration. I remember back when I was only 6 years old going to do volunteer and fundraising work at the University of Calgary. My mom has lived a life of giving back and I want to do the same.

Has your life changed as a result of being a Better Human? Tell me how.

My life has definitely changed since I started giving back. I feel less greedy and absolutely love the impact I can have on others by simply doing things for them. Also, when you give back you get a release of endorphins, the happiness drug in your brain. What a great thing to be addicted to, giving back to others.

Tell me why young people can make a difference in the world if they take action.

Teens can make a difference because they have the intelligence and are typically motivated to make the world a better place.

Steve's Reflections

I connected with Izzy indirectly through my wife, and then with Izzy's her mom. My discussion with Izzy was highlighted by her passion for others. We met over the phone so I could not see her face, but I could hear the passion in her voice about volunteering. It's very clear that Izzy has one main plan in life; help other people! I was struck by her story of helping others and especially understanding the importance of empathy when dealing with others who are not as fortunate. Izzy has very specific future plans to give back and not surprisingly, the scope of her plans has no borders. Izzy is on the way to change the world!

Stories Compiled by Melissa From

Uplift to Be Uplifted

At the age of 16 Amelia decided to take matters into her own hands to change the competitive culture in her school into a culture of team-work and helping others succeed - both in and out of the classroom.

What does it mean to be a Better Human?

A popular piece of advice I have been given is "Don't compare yourself to others", but I think that is a little unfinished. In addition to not discrediting yourself by comparing yourself to others, I think it is important to compare your current self to your past self. The "better" part of "being a Better Human" means being a better version of yourself.

To me, the word "human" suggests responsibility. As humans, we owe a responsibility to humanity, to helping others who are less fortunate, to protecting every culture and language, to standing up for the rights we ought to have and the values we believe in. As a human, we also owe our responsibility to other species and the Earth we live on, to protect the environment, to help endangered animals, to keep the Earth as close to how we found it as possible for those who come after us.

Together, I think to be a Better Human means to take action, big or small, with those responsibilities in mind, and to do it better than yesterday.

Why is it important to you?

The environments I find myself in are becoming increasingly competitive and difficult, whether that is transitioning from high school to university, or extracurricular activities to internships. The competitiveness and difficulty can sometimes make me lose sight of what the ultimate goals of some of these endeavors are. I think "to be a Better Human" serves as a reminder to help others and to do more because there is always room to do better.

Tell me a story about a time when you did something to be a Better Human. What was the impact of that? How did it make you feel?

I attend a very competitive academic high school in my city. There was tutoring available at the school to assist students, but the existing program seemed to only increase the competition and divide in the student body.

This cut-throat competition and its negative consequences inspired me to start the student-run organization, *Uplift*, where senior students volunteer to provide free tutoring to junior students. I recruited a team of 12 executives and 20 volunteers, serving over 200 participants. We help students build solid academic foundations by teaching Grade 10 courses to Grade 9 students over the summer. We help students gain stronger conceptual understanding and problem-solving skills. In addition, we post weekly blogs and host regular information sessions to share tips and opportunities that promote a stronger school community.

As freshmen at my high school, our participants are already acting as strong leaders of the community. In addition to excelling in class, they take communal responsibilities one step further by helping others academically and socially.

This experience showed me the power I have to impact and influence others and allowed me to feel the joy that is unique to helping others.

What is something specific you want to do to be a Better Human?

I have an immigrant story similar to many others. I came to Canada in grade four and was given the support of many kind individuals in the community. I have always been looking for ways to do the same for others now that I have become immersed in the local culture and community. Currently, I am working on a subtitle initiative that works with English content creators to add subtitles in multiple languages. Watching a video multiple times with subtitles in both my native language and English was a highly effective way for me to learn conversational English; however, finding resources that contained both subtitles was rather difficult. I want to start a subtitling organization that will produce more language learning material for people who are new to English-speaking countries.

What advice would you give to other teens if they want to be Better Humans today?

Never underestimate the impact of your actions. As a young person, it is normal to feel powerless. As long as you are taking positive action with the good of others in mind, it will reach people. For whoever you reach, that small act of kindness may have a very strong and meaningful impact.

Don't feel like you have to start something all on your own. If you are unsure where to start, try to join existing initiatives that are related to your interests.

Tell me about a time when you failed trying to be a Better Human and what you did.

After a round of a debate competition, some friends and I witnessed a debater get berated, insulted and embarrassed by her partner. This person clearly thought it was her teammate's fault that their team performed poorly. I knew that I should say something, but was afraid to because no one else was saying anything. Eventually, a debater from another team spoke up and brought the issue to the attention of the tournament's Equity Officer.

The issue was dealt with and we all learned a valuable lesson about how to treat others and about speaking up when we see injustice.

This experience reminds me to stand up for others whenever I can.

What's been your greatest challenge and how did you overcome that challenge to be a Better Human?

As an introvert, I am motivated to work for good causes but I worry about how I will convince others to get involved to help. With the support of others in my community, I have learned to advocate for my ideas and encourage others to join initiatives

I am passionate about. I have learned to speak up about issues in my community. The hardest thing was taking the first step. Once I spoke up once, I realized that people want to do good and they want to help.

Is there something/someone that inspires you to be a Better Human? What is it that inspires you?

My mom inspires me to be a Better Human because she always takes the time to help others despite juggling many commitments. She is generous and supportive. She always considers matters from other peoples' perspectives. At the same time, she is not afraid to say no to things that are against her values. Once she is sure of something, she gives it her full effort, which is something that I admire and hope to achieve.

Has your life changed as a result of being a Better Human? Tell me how.

Being a Better Human has allowed me to see so much more kindness in the world. I notice the things, big or small, that everyday people do to make the world a better place. These things give me a lot of motivation to help others. Being a Better Human has allowed me to feel the joy and fulfillment of volunteering my time and bringing kindness into the lives of others. It has given me the opportunity to grow as a leader and to encourage more people in taking positive action in support of the causes they believe in.

The more I do, the more opportunities I see. I see the gaps and I see where I can fit in and do things to help out.

Tell me why young people can make a difference in the world if they take action.

Youth can encourage and motivate other youth in a way that adults cannot. By taking action, young people can start a movement. Young people often set trends in society through social media and pop culture. We have the capacity to influence and shape the values of society if we channel our efforts appropriately.

Melissa's Reflections

Amelia was recommended to me by a friend of hers for this project. I think that one of the highest honours we can obtain is to be seen by our peers as someone who is making a difference. Amelia was incredibly humble through our conversation, but as a young immigrant she has contributed so much to the culture of her community and school. Amelia is seen as someone who wants to make things better and who is willing to put in the work it takes to get it done.

I'm a Big Fan

After seeing a news story about low income seniors suffering through the hot Texas summer without air conditioning or even a fan to cool them off, Paige took it upon herself to collect new and gently used fans to help them beat the heat.

What does it mean to be a Better Human?

A lot of young people just like to complain about the situation but they don't do anything about it. I want to be a person who takes action. When I see a problem, I want to be part of the solution.

Why is it important to you?

My family has always been active in the community through volunteerism. We volunteer together once a month. This is a value that has been instilled in me by my parents and they have really empowered me and helped me to see that it is not just adults who can make a difference.

Tell me a story about a time when you did something to be a Better Human. What was the impact of that? How did it make you feel?

I heard a story on the news about seniors struggling with the heat in the Texas summer. A lot of them are on a fixed income and don't have air conditioning and can't even afford a fan. It can be incredibly hot here in the summer and I can't imagine living in this heat without something to cool off my living space.

I took it on myself to collect new/used fans from family and friends in the area. I worked with the local Fire Department to identify seniors and low income families who would benefit from these donated fans.

It's not really a big deal to ask a few people for the donation of a new or used fan, but it made a big difference for these people. It made me feel really good to be able to help them.

What is something specific you want to do to be a Better Human?

I want to continue to do more in the community. When I grow up and have a family, I will probably follow my parents' example and have my children volunteer in the community too. I think that it is really important to instill those values from a young age.

What advice would you give to other teens if they want to be Better Humans today?

I would tell other teens to just step up and take action. Find a charity and just start volunteering. As young people, we get used to being told what to do, so we just sit and wait to be told to volunteer or do something to help out. I want to encourage my peers to stop waiting for someone to tell you to do it - take initiative!

What has stopped you from taking action to be a Better Human in the past?

I work, go to school and participate in extracurricular activities so it can be hard to find the time to volunteer and give back if I don't make it a priority.

Tell me about a time when you failed trying to be a Better Human and what you did.

I had an assignment, through Girl Scouts, to volunteer with a women's shelter. I had a special project all planned out, and then they told me they didn't want to use volunteers. I was really discouraged and unmotivated. I had to find another charity to work with.

In the end, I did find another charity to get involved with and it was an even better fit for me and I had a lot of fun working with them. It was a really fulfilling experience. It was a good reminder not to give up and also that giving back and volunteering is not always easy.

What's been your greatest challenge and how did you overcome that challenge to be a Better Human?

Follow through on volunteering can be challenging. There are often competing priorities. I use my day timer and I schedule time to volunteer so I make sure it happens. It's important to me to make it a priority and not just something I talk about.

Is there something/someone that inspires you to be a Better Human? What is it that inspires you?

I am really fortunate to have a group of friends and family who are really community minded. It's important to surround yourself with people who support you and share in your passions.

I don't know that I could say any single person inspires me more than the others. My entire group of friends and family are all very giving and generous and inspire me in different ways.

Has your life changed as a result of being a Better Human? Tell me how.

Definitely! When I was younger, giving back and getting involved in volunteering was something I did because I had to. Now I do it because I want to. Also, I have evolved to the point where I am instigating volunteer opportunities and ways of giving back instead of waiting for someone else to create those opportunities for me.

Tell me why young people can make a difference in the world if they take action.

As young people, we have the opportunities to make a significant impact on today's world problems. We have our whole lives ahead of us and the younger we start, the more impact we can have. If you want something to be different in the world, in your community, in your school, or even in your own house - take the initiative to make it happen. Stop waiting for someone else to be the hero. You ARE the hero, put on the cape and get to work!

Melissa's Reflections

I went to school with Paige's mom from grade 1 all the way through grade 12. It is no surprise to me that Paige is an active volunteer. As a young person, Paige's mom was a Girl Guide and was often involved in charitable endeavors. Paige mentions in her interview that her family volunteers together. Speaking with Paige was a stark reminder to me as a parent that I have the opportunity and responsibility to model being a Better Human for my children. It is amazing to think that acts of kindness and community involvement may not only impact your community today, but you could be creating generations of impact through the behaviours that you role model.

It's a Birthday Miracle

At the age of 13 Sheliza decided to use her birthday to bring attention and resources to a local charity. At 15 she started her own charity to make sure that every child is celebrated on their birthday.

What does it mean to be a Better Human?

To me, being a Better Human is being an individual who identifies a problem and finds a practical solution. I think it is especially great if you can engage others in the process or solution.

Why is it important to you?

I truly believe that we are placed on this earth to give back. I have learned that I can make a big impact by doing small things.

When I travelled internationally, I saw how privileged I have been and this gave me a new found gratitude for the life I have. It also instilled in me the need to use my privilege to do more for others.

Tell me a story about a time when you did something to be a Better Human. What was the impact of that? How did it make you feel?

On my 12th birthday, I suffered a severe allergic reaction that resulted in an emergency trip to the hospital. I was pretty devastated that my party was basically ruined by this. My mom pointed out that there are kids around the world who don't even get birthday parties. In fact, there were other 12 years olds in my own city who would never know what it was like to have a birthday party. This was an incredible reality check for me.

The following year, for my 13th birthday, instead of having a party for myself, I did some research online about local charities that helped kids and families. I found one that I like and I rallied a bunch of my friends and family to go and host a pancake breakfast for all of the families and children staying at a local emergency shelter. It was amazing! I did this again for my 14th and 15th birthdays.

On my 16th birthday I took it a bit further and I asked the emergency shelter if I could hold a birthday party at their centre. From there we started a "Party it Forward" program, where other kids could use their own birthday to raise money for the shelter's kids to have birthday parties and presents.

This resulted in me founding Children's Birthday Miracles, a Canadian registered charity, dedicated to providing birthday experiences to children whose families cannot afford gifts or parties.

In the beginning In the beginning this was a small initiative. My family and I did everything. Now, through our "Party It Forward" program, we are offering the opportunity for other children and teens to give back as well.

I just feel so good to be doing something to help others. And, it feels even better to help others help others.

A close friend of mine passed away a few years ago and I started to host birthday parties for kids with cancer in his honour. That has been a really healing experience for me in a lot of ways. Giving back and doing good helps me as much as it helps the people I am serving.

What is something specific you want to do to be a Better Human?

I just finished my Engineering degree and I want to find a way to use my technical skills to help others. I think that I can have the most impact if I find ways to give back that use my strengths.

What advice would you give to other teens if they want to be Better Humans today?

Figure out what you are most passionate about. In order to do this, you are going to have to explore everything and experiment a bit. Try volunteering with a few different charities until you find the right fit.

When you can align your skills and passions in volunteering, that is when the real magic happens.

What has stopped you from taking action to be a Better Human in the past? Why?

Definitely my age.

I was young when I started volunteering and not much older when I started Children's Birthday Miracles. I would reach out to companies to ask for donations, or try to book meetings with emergency shelters to bring birthday parties to more under-privileged kids and people wouldn't take my call or they would question whether I should be doing this given my age. It was really discouraging sometimes, but also empowering. I felt really good about proving people wrong and showing that a young person could actually start a charity and make it work.

Tell me about a time when you failed trying to be a Better Human and what you did.

A lot of my experience relates to Children's Birthday Miracles because I put a lot of my time and effort into that initiative. But, it wasn't always smooth sailing. After a few years of working with the same emergency shelter to provide birthday parties and gifts to children, the shelter started to shift priorities and we were no longer a good fit. My first reaction was to assume that this was the end of my charity. I was pretty devastated. But, there were still plenty of underserved children in my city, I just needed to shift my focus and find them.

I was able to establish new partnerships with different organizations and overcome the obstacle of that initial rejection. It was a really good lesson in resilience. Just because you are doing something good, or something you see as good, doesn't mean that everyone else will see the value or that it will be easy. In fact, it can actually be a lot of hard work. But, part of the reward is in pushing through.

What's been your greatest challenge and how did you overcome that challenge to be a Better Human?

My age was a pretty big challenge. I was really young - and I looked and sounded young - when I started, and people didn't really believe that I was capable of doing all of this. There was a lot of judgement and negativity surrounding that.

I do think that is shifting in society a bit and there is more openness to letting teens step up and be engaged.

Is there something/someone that inspires you to be a Better Human? What is it that inspires you?

My mom is definitely the reason I am what I am. She is a social worker. She immigrated to Canada as a young person and is very grateful for the life we have here. She really instilled a sense of giving back since I was young. She was very pivotal in pushing me to keep going when I faced obstacles with Children's Birthday Miracles. She made sure that I kept a positive outlook.

What has been the impact of being a Better Human on you?

My life has changed significantly. I have experienced the joys and personal satisfaction of giving back, but I have also had to learn to overcome the challenges too.

It has been really incredible to have the chance to engage others and to give them the chance to be Better Humans too.

Tell me why young people can make a difference in the world if they take action.

I think young people can make a huge difference. We see the world and all of its problems through a fresh set of eyes in a lot of ways. Young people are often creative and have great ideas and solutions to the problems our communities face. And, to be honest, we are a little less busy and have time to give as well. A little less time online and a little more time helping others is a sacrifice that most young people can make.

Melissa's Reflections

I have known Sheliza since she was 14 years old. I have had a front row seat to the creation and success for Children's Birthday Miracles. Sheliza has thrown herself into the success of that organization and the mission behind it. She worked tirelessly to complete high school, and then a 4 year university degree, while running and growing the organization. From Sheliza I have learned the value of hardwork. Giving back and doing good is not always easy, but it is always worth it.

Agent of Change

At 18, Sahil has already dedicated himself to be an agent of change in his school and his community.

What does it mean to be a Better Human?

I think being a Better Human is about having a positive impact on the community and basic aspects of citizenship. It doesn't have to be a big grandiose action. It is about the everyday mundane things. It can be small. It can become a habit. It can be almost addicting.

Why is it important to you?

We need people to be agents of change. Service and citizenship are important, but not everyone is thinking about this. If you see a problem, don't wait for someone else to take care of it. It's a bit like being an entrepreneur – think about what you want to see in the future and then go and create it. Everyone has the ability to ask "What can I do RIGHT NOW?"

Tell me a story about a time when you did something to be a Better Human. What was the impact of that? How did it make you feel?

I have been really fortunate to have amazing mentors in my life. Some are adults, but some are actually other teenagers who I really respect and admire. Mentorship is really important to me.

In the fall, one of my peers reached out to me for advice. We went for coffee and just talked through what was going on. It wasn't much out of my day, but my past experience allowed me to really help her in a big way. She was able to take some of my advice and use it. It helped her and her team at Cadets in the long run. Everyone has a unique skill and it isn't much to share that with others.

It felt good. It was almost addicting. It made me want to do more. It made me want to go out and foster more relationships like that.

What is something specific you want to do to be a Better Human?

I want to learn to listen better. At the end of the day, if I want to have a bigger impact on the community, I need to be able to listen and be a shoulder for others to lean on. Sometimes you just need to be able to listen.

What advice would you give to other teens if they want to be Better Humans today?

It is important to be empathetic. Going into high school, I was oblivious about what was going on in other people's lives. It was all about me. It was kind of eye opening to realize there is this whole world out there that has nothing to do with me.

Sometimes it's simple things, like asking other people what meeting time works for them instead of just stating a time. Other times, it is asking a friend how they are doing and then asking again, "No, how are you *really* doing?", and then just listening.

What has stopped you from taking action to be a Better Human in the past?

In the past, I have failed to be empathetic and consider what is going on in other people's lives. Even when I was working on worthwhile charitable initiatives, my efforts were hindered by my inability to consider the others on my team. Once you learn to consider other viewpoints and experiences, it really helps you to take action in a more effective way. It is a really powerful thing.

Tell me about a time when you failed trying to be a Better Human and what you did.

There was a situation a year ago where I should have stepped in. We were trying to arrange rides for a group of us to go to volunteer at a charity fundraiser. I wasn't really considering the needs of others. Not everyone had access to public transit and I failed to consider their perspective. Everyone was volunteering for charity, but there was this barrier of how to get everyone there. People got frustrated and we lost some volunteers.

What's been your greatest challenge and how did you overcome that challenge to be a Better Human?

The greatest challenge that I have is to admit when I have made a mistake. I ramble and make excuses. But, it is really just so much easier to own it. You have to admit you are wrong in order to make a better game plan for next time. By owning your mistakes, you become more trustworthy.

Is there something/someone that inspires you to be a Better Human? What is it that inspires you?

As I mentioned earlier, mentorship is really important to me. Another teen who I look up to in my school has really inspired me. He is older than me and took me under his wing and mentored me. His approach was very subtle and didn't make me feel small. He was so kind to everyone in the school and he was always volunteering - I wanted to be like that!

I encourage young teens to find a role model in high school. Try to be like that person. On the other side of that, I encourage older teens to find a younger teen to connect with and mentor. When you mentor someone else, you inevitably get something out of that relationship too.

Has your life changed as a result of being a Better Human? Tell me how.

I used to just do my school work and call it a day. As I spent more time with quality people who were doing a lot to make our school and our city a better place, I started to see opportunities to use my skills to help out. As I began to have a positive impact on my school and community, I wanted to do more. It is amazing how good it feels to do good things. I have realized that it often doesn't take much time and effort to make a difference.

Tell me why young people can make a difference in the world if they take action.

We, as young people, have a new and different perspective that adults don't have. We can be agents of change.

I think there is a surge in political activism. Young people have a unique take on the world and we can take action to have our voices heard.

Melissa's Reflections

Sahil is such a great example of a young person who is living every day of his life to be a Better Human Teenager. It is not in the big grandiose gestures, but in the little everyday acts of kindness that Sahil carves out a better corner of the world. It takes time and commitment to establish these habits. Sahil admits he still has to be conscious in his actions and words on a daily basis, but he also confirmed that it does get easier.

From Trials to Triumph

At 17 years old, Zarek started volunteering with the very organization that he credits with changing his life.

What does it mean to be a Better Human?

I think that being a Better Human is all about giving back. I have had a pretty rough life, especially as a kid and young teenager, but I have also experienced the support and help of some amazing people. I know first hand that just one person caring, helping, and showing support can make all the difference.

Why is it important to you?

I am who I am today because someone cared enough to help me. I want to be that person for other young people. I want to be that person for my own son.

Tell me a story about a time when you did something to be a Better Human. What was the impact of that? How did it make you feel?

I have been involved with a local Indigenous youth charity that really helped me through some tough circumstances. In recent years, I have been able to volunteer with that same organization. I have helped to mentor other teens, I have organized youth activities, I have helped to collect winter coats for homeless teens.

It feels really good to give back. I think it feels especially good for me to pay it forward within the organization that really helped me.

What is something specific you want to do to be a Better Human?

I want to continue to be involved with the youth and organizations I am currently working with. I plan to go to film school and I want to find a way to combine my passion for the arts and for vulnerable young people. I think there can be a lot of healing through artistic expression. I want to help others find their voice through that.

What advice would you give to other teens if they want to be Better Humans today?

Look around you. There might be someone in your school, maybe even in your friendship circle, who is really hurting. A lot of my friends at school didn't know what I was dealing with at home. Being a Better Human doesn't have to be a big initiative or anything fancy. It might be sharing your sandwich with the kids who don't have lunch.

What has stopped you from taking action to be a Better Human in the past?

I faced a lot of obstacles growing up. I was raised in a home that was very abusive. Neglect and domestic violence was a regular occurrence. When I finally had enough and left, I found myself homeless at the age of 16. After several months of being homeless, and falling into more dysfunctional and problematic situations I found myself in a youth shelter. I was placed there by a well meaning Social Worker.

What most people don't realize is how rough those environments can be. A bunch of kids from bad family situations that have usually involved a lot of violence and substance abuse are put all together. There can tend to be a lot of drug use in those places. Unfortunately, I went from an abusive home situation, to being homeless, to having some very serious drug addiction and substance abuse problems. As you can imagine, all of this had a serious impact on my mental health.

When you are facing obstacle after obstacle in your life, it can be pretty hard to see past that to look at how you can give back or help. I needed some of my basic human needs to be met first before I could give back.

One amazing thing that came out of all of that though, was that I became involved with this organization called USAY (Urban Society for Aborginal Youth). USAY gave me a safe place. I found connections there. People cared about me and I started to find myself caring about them too. From there it was a natural progression to overcome the years of hurt to bring myself to a place where and I could give back.

Tell me about a time when you failed trying to be a Better Human and what you did.

There was a period of a few months, 2 years ago, when I lost 13 different friends and family members to substance abuse or suicide. I really felt like I had failed through that time. I failed to connect with people, to help them, to get them the help they needed. But, through that experience, I also learned that you can only help people when they are ready and want to be helped.

What's been your greatest challenge and how did you overcome that challenge to be a Better Human?

This is a hard question for me. As I have mentioned, I have experienced a lot of challenges. I am not sure that I overcame all of them, but I got through them. Looking back on it now, I can see that a lot of the hardship; the abuse, the addiction, the homelessness, has made me who I am. These things have made me sensitive to the hardships and the needs of others.

Is there something/someone that inspires you to be a Better Human? What is it that inspires you?

I have positive influences and negative influences that help to inspire me. My girlfriend is an incredibly positive role model for me. She is so selfless and so giving. She has helped me so much on my journey.

In my childhood and early teen years I experienced some negative influences. Those experiences and individuals helped me see what I don't want to do and who I don't want to become.

And, finally, my son is a great inspiration to me. Becoming a parent as a teenager is hard. It is really important to me that I provide the stability, security, and love that I didn't have and that my son deserves. I am inspired every day to do right by him.

Has your life changed as a result of being a Better Human? Tell me how.

I am much less selfish than I used to be. I can see how my actions and choices affect others. When I started to volunteer with USAY, I saw other young people coming from similar situations to mine. Helping others has helped me to work through the pain of my own past.

Tell me why young people can make a difference in the world if they take action.

I am living proof that a simple act of kindness can change a person's life. And when you change one person's life, you change the lives of everyone that person goes on to affect.

Melissa's Reflections

I was introduced to Zarek through my friends at the Calgary based non-profit organization, Youth Central. Tarek has a reputation in the city of Calgary for his incredible generosity, commitment to giving back, and for doing this all despite the obstacles he has faced in his life. Tarek is an example of turning a bad situation into something good. This didn't just happen though. It took Better Humans being there for Tarek along the way, for him to see this role modeled. And, it took Tarek making a commitment to himself and to those around him that he was going to be a Better Human and break the cycle.

Stories compiled by
Paul Lamoureux

You Have the Power to Inspire!

Sarah Zuo believes everybody has the capacity to take action, initiate change, and make things better! She is a hard-working and creative student who strongly believes in youth empowerment and community engagement. She acts as an executive member in several school clubs and local youth initiatives. In her free time she enjoys moving, grooving, and rewatching her favourite Broadway musicals (Chicago and Dear Evan Hansen). Her favourite piece of advice – it's always better to be overdressed.

What does it mean to be a Better Human?

For me, being a Better Human means to always be authentic – I should always strive to be who I *am* instead of who I think I should be. It is also more than showing up and voicing my opinions. Being a Better Human means to create space for others to show up as well. I am proud of my passions, but I have also learned to set boundaries. My "yes" is meaningless unless I also know how to say "no." It is so important to keep an open mindset for growth and to embrace curiosity just for the sake of curiosity. I recognize my strengths and how I can use my strengths to support the people around me. However, I also know when to ask for help when I need it. Better Humans are leaders, but leadership is not a synonym for dictatorship. Great leaders support their team from behind and strive to give others the chance to grow as well.

Why is it important to be a Better Human?

We all have infinite potential, and it is up to us how far we want to take our potential. What you do matters. What I do matters. We all matter, and can do incredible things that matter together. Every single action leaves an impact. Sometimes, that impact is tangible and easy to see. Other times, it is hard to realize how much you have affected somebody else in ways you cannot even imagine. Better Humans create impact everywhere they go. Either in the form of a kind word to a peer or a radical idea that greatly moves their community, interacting with the world around us can open up endless opportunities. The only way for us to end up creating tangible change is to believe we can and to not be afraid to challenge the status quo.

My mother has always told me to strive for excellence, in myself and in everything I do. I am willing to explore my boundaries and push my edges for the sake of bettering myself, to become my most authentic self. It is so important to be a Better Human, not as a noun, but as an adjective. There is no ideal Better Human, there is only inspiration, determination, and self-reflection.

Tell me a story about a time when you did something to be a Better Human. What was the impact of that? How did it make you feel? Did you have any challenges?

I grew up in Shanghai under the care of my grandparents, aunt, and uncle. My mother was a pre-professional dancer back in her day, and so she ensured that I was raised with a love for dance. I have been a dancer for as long as I can remember, starting with ballet at age three, and expanding into different forms of dance such as jazz, acrobatics, and contemporary. Dance has always been a passion of mine, but it is so much more than a hobby. Back when my mom lived 11,415 km away in Toronto, ON I only got to see her for a limited time every summer. During those precious weeks, the majority of our time together was spent in the studio, she mentored me in ballet and worked with me tirelessly. I distinctly remember practicing the Petit Jeté over a hundred times, and throughout all the practices, my mom always remained my biggest challenger - and yet my supporter.

In my dance class, the teacher usually chose a demonstrator after each exercise. Before that summer, I was never picked, and none of the other parents ever noticed me. However, after my mom's invaluable guidance, I started to be picked to be the demonstrator more and more. One class, I even demonstrated every single exercise over the course of the two-hour class! The other parents gushed over my improvement, but my mom never took credit. She insisted that my improvement was the result of my own hard work.

Dance taught me the values of perseverance, dedication, and purpose. Being in such a high-stress environment with rehearsals up to 10 hours a day gave me a second family whom I could communicate with without words, who shared my sense of purpose, and understood the mental and physical exhaustion of a dancer.

Last year, I was lucky enough to be given an opportunity to pass on this passion. One day, at the end of my ballet vocational class, my teacher briefly mentioned that her next class – full of sixteen energetic eleven-year-olds – was a lot to handle and she wished she had an assistant in the class. All the other kids nodded sympathetically, but I was the only one who stayed after class and asked if I could help in any way. Delighted, she agreed, and I began volunteering weekly after my regular classes. I now assist a junior ballet class with 16 little girls who all dream of wearing pink tutus, buying their first pair of pointe shoes, and stepping out on stage for the first time. They take my corrections with grateful smiles and inspire me just as much as I hope to inspire them.

What is something specific you want to do to be a Better Human?

I need to give people the benefit of the doubt in assuming that they are trying their best. I always joke that I exist best in a state of constant high stress – the more things I need to get done, the better I end up planning out my day and utilizing my time efficiently. However, I need to remember that everybody's threshold for stress is different. Interacting with people under the empathetic mindset that they are currently doing their very best eliminates a lot of the stress that stems from our own insecurities. When your best friend complains about a project or an assignment that you found easy, you would never judge them. You want to help them to be better, and this is the mindset we need to carry over to every person in our lives. Just because someone is struggling a little in an area that you thrived in does not mean that they have less capacity to learn and grow than you.

I was taught this lesson by a close friend of mine who has known me since grade school. We were working together on an important project pitch, and one of the other girls seemed to only be there out of convenience. She was working on a task for another project, and I remember feeling frustrated that she was not actively contributing like the rest of the team. Afterward, I expressed my frustration to my friend, and she told me that the other girl just started working a very stressful job. Suddenly, I felt very guilty. Instead of focusing on myself and wallowing in frustration, I should have put myself in her shoes. I should have reached out and asked how she was feeling with her new job, and how I could help, instead of brushing off her stress in my mind and comparing her to myself. Empathy and understanding are some of the greatest gifts we can give to others, and in order for me to become a Better Human, I need to accept all the Better Humans already all around me.

What advice would you give to teens if they want to be Better Humans today?

There is an ancient Chinese fable called The Frog of the Well. The story goes:

There once was a frog who lived down a little well. The Frog was so content with his home that he never came out. He had no awareness of the outside world. All the Frog did, day after day, was sit on a lily pad at the bottom of the well, and appreciate the sky above his well. He had no idea what existed outside of his world. One day, a turtle walked by and peeked into the well. He asked the Frog, "What are you doing down here? I'm heading to the ocean." The frog had never heard of the ocean before. He had never seen anything outside of the small circle of blue sky. He asked the turtle what the ocean was. The turtle replied "The ocean? It's paradise." And the frog, for the first time in his life, decided to leave his well for a whole new world outside.

I love this fable because one of the most important lessons you can learn is that not knowing where you're heading is okay. As teenagers, we are in that stage in our lives where we're trying to figure out who we are, and who we want to be. We are constantly told that we need to decide on a dream, to spend our time accumulating one passion. We are praised so much for having a destination when we should be proud of our journey. So go take initiative. If you recognize a problem around you – whether it is a social challenge or a resource barrier – do something about it. People are always willing to help you if you reach out, and always remember to thank and appreciate the people that are willing to help you on your way there.

It's important to realize that the strengths that make you who you are today are going to remain within your core tomorrow, or perhaps in 10 years from now. You have to trust that what makes you great today is still going to make you great years from now. It's really important to be mindful of focusing too much on the end goal, when the important part is the journey to get there. If you are too focused, you may miss out on other more important opportunities. By planning out every aspect of your life, what you are actually doing is denying yourself opportunities to grow.

What's been your greatest challenge and how did you overcome that challenge to be a Better Human?

Last year, my math teacher reached out to me and my co-founder of a youth initiative for a chance to speak at the annual University of Calgary Leadership Conference. We had talked to her about our organization's mission and vision many times before, and she thought the conference was a perfect fit for our values. The conference was usually only open to UofC faculty, students, and parents, but she encouraged us to apply anyways. We sent over a brief outline of what impact we wished to create in 40 minutes, and to our delight, we were picked to head a morning workshop – Student Leadership: How to Approach Issues Important to You – on our initiative promoting workplace readiness in youth. There were six other workshops all running during the exact same time slot as our presentation, and we were terrified that not a single person would show up. By 9:40 AM, we were proven very wrong.

I vividly remember standing in front of the projector and waiting for the last few stragglers to trickle in when I finally realized that I was standing in front of a room full of university students. I had taken on this opportunity without batting an eyelash and without considering just how qualified I actually was to inspire a room full of young adults. We presented and left the last twenty minutes open for networking and connecting – integral lessons we emphasized during our speech. To my surprise, people began flocking to the front of the room to where we were, thanking us for the incredible story of our journey, failures, and successes. Many asked where they could find us on campus, why we were not an official UofC club, or even wondering if we could extend our mission to high-schoolers. Nobody had even realized that we were in high-school, and nobody thought less of us.

This conference made me realize that no matter how old you are, you have the power to inspire! My biggest challenge was the barrier I placed over myself. Imposter Syndrome is something we all struggle with at times, especially when we feel like the only one in a room. Either physically or intellectually, if you have ever felt like an outlier at some point, turn that into your greatest strength. Don't think, "Am I good enough to be here?" Instead, recognize that your voice is needed the most. So don't settle for fitting in. Instead, aspire to belong.

Is there something/someone that inspires you to be a Better Human? What is it that inspires you?

Someone once told me that you are the average of the five closest people to you. I really love this quote, because your idols should be people you know in your life. We often look up to figureheads and celebrities, but we only see their successes and not their failures. I am inspired every single day by my family and my friends. When a friend brings me a coffee because I seemed stressed, or offers to give me a ride after practice, it inspires me just as much as a powerful presentation. Inspiration should not only stem from grand gestures or innovations that have radically changed the world. We should be inspired to be kind, to be empathetic, and to make the people in our lives feel important. Let's normalize the word "idol," because we can all be idols.

Failure is something we need to embrace, especially when we are young. When you are a teenager, or just transitioning out of your teenage years, you are in the prime position to bounce back from failure. It is so much better to try and fail when you are just beginning, then to invest decades of work into a project you have since realized that is not your passion at all. Furthermore, failure is more than starting a project and having it not succeed in the way you anticipated. Failure is also staying in a place where you're not really happy, but you make do because you're scared to "fail" in the dictionary definition. You may have not lost any capital, but is that worth failing yourself?

Has your life changed as a result of being a Better Human? Tell me how.

Being a Better Human inspires me to chase the heartbeat moments and chase after my passions. The growth mindset of being a Better Human allows me to accept failures and take them in stride. You should not turn down an opportunity because you're afraid to fail. Instead, you should believe in yourself the way your parents or your best friend believes in you. Whenever I am given an opportunity, I see it as a learning experience. Even if your application gets rejected, or your interview flops, now you know what not to do for next time. Knowing what doesn't work is just important and recognizing what works. There is no set path to success, there is only perseverance and a willingness to take the next step.

I am not sure who I am yet, but I am excited to find out.

Tell me why young people can make a difference in the world if they take action.

This past summer, I participated in a summer program called SHAD, a STREAM and entrepreneurship program for youths across Canada. As a part of this program, we got keynote sessions with some incredible people. Included were Dr. Donna Strickland – a Nobel Prize Winner in Physics, Michele Romanow from Dragon's Den, and many other notable names. Reading their bios, I was initially very intimidated by how successful they all were. However, after listening to their stories, I have realized that what makes them figures of inspiration were not their stories of success. It was also the recounting of their various failures.

They all started out as youths just like us. They applied to the universities we are planning to apply to, they did similar clubs and activities in high school, so what prevents us from being just as successful as them? One day, we could be those speakers! The only difference between our dreams and our successes is action: action to be okay with looking silly, action and willingness to explore, action to be okay with a step forward, no matter how small that step is. Youths are the future of the world, and it is time we start believing that.

Paul's Reflections

There were so many take-aways from this conversation with Sarah. Her enthusiasm for being a Better Human shone through but what stood out the most was her message of courage and the need to embrace uncertainty. The courage to seek out failure and realize that "what doesn't work is just as important as recognizing what works. There is no set path to success, not knowing where you are heading is okay" - this message is so important for teens. She inspires teens to be courageous and realize that, "The only difference between our dreams and our successes is action." Sarah also expressed a deep understanding that "Empathy and understanding are some of the greatest gifts we can give to others" and that "no matter how old you are, you have the power to inspire!"

Just wow!

The Love for Poppa

Owen is a grade 8 student, on the west coast of Canada. He enjoys reading and playing video games. Owen has been fundraising for cancer research since he was five, and is still passionate about the subject. Owen enjoys winter, and loves the snow. He enjoys school and spending time with his friends. In the future, Owen hopes to continue being a Better Human, and helping others the best he can.

What does it mean to be a Better Human?

To be a Better Human is to sacrifice your own time for other people, with, or without benefit for yourself. It means to create positive relationships with other people, in your community, or across the world. It could be a simple act from a compliment, to fundraising for a cause you believe in.

At home you can help out your parents by doing chores, helping other kids who are struggling in school - try to teach them instead of simply giving them the answer. Courage is important - having the courage to talk, speak up, and decide to do something positive.

Why is it important to be a Better Human?

It is important to be a Better Human, because you are helping other people. Making people happy is an important thing, and when people are happy, they work better, may help you, and help out others more often. Being a Better Human makes me happy, because I know I am bringing joy to other people. It positively helps other people who will in turn help other people. It helps improve their mood. My parents showed me how important it is to be positive when helping out around the house. It showed me how it made me happy when I was helping them and we can show other kids the same.

Tell me a story about a time when you did something to be a Better Human. What was the impact of that? How did it make you feel? Did you have any challenges?

One thing I have done to be a Better Human was to start fundraising for the Island Prostate Centre when my Poppa was diagnosed with prostate cancer. I was only 5 years old when I started. My birthday wish on my 5th birthday was to make my Poppa's cancer go away. I wanted to do this because I was worried for my Poppa and I knew that in some way my fundraising could benefit him and all the other people with prostate cancer. Through my fundraising I have raised $25,000 to aid in support and research for prostate cancer. My fundraising has also brought more awareness to prostate cancer and may have saved many lives. Doing all this fundraising and awareness has made me feel really happy that I was helping other people. I am very proud of myself seeing that just as a kid I can make a positive impact on others' lives.

With the support of my family, my Poppa specifically, and the Island Prostate Centre in Victoria, BC, as well as my friends and schools, I have been able to overcome challenges such as where I could fundraise, how to create awareness and how to raise money. At first I was nervous, I wondered if anyone would help me with it, and after my first goal of raising $100 was reached I saw how easy it could be to make a difference.

My parents helped me get started. I sold some toys, donated money from my birthday and from Santa, my family did bottle drives, I sold freezies, family and friends donated money, and I spoke at a school assembly where my mom was working. From there, awareness grew and anonymous people started donating money under my name on the Island Prostate Centre website. My big challenge was how to actually raise money and raise awareness.

My fear at first was that people would not understand how important this was to me and not donate any money. Public speaking was a little bit scary but after I spoke in front of a large group of kids at the school assembly I realized that I wasn't afraid to do more.

What is something specific you want to do to be a Better Human?

Something I would like to do to be a Better Human is to continue to think of the needs of others before myself and continue raising awareness for causes I believe in like the Island Prostate Centre.

What advice would you give to teens if they want to be Better Humans today?

Advice I would give to teens to be Better Humans is to think about your actions before you do them, and always consider the impact they will have on others. Always try and build people up, instead of breaking them down. When people are happy mentally and physically, they will be a Better Human too.

One day I received a letter from an anonymous person who explained how my actions really made a difference in their lives and they donated $50 to me. This really showed me how much my actions were in fact making a difference. Teens need to have the confidence to know that their actions, no matter how small, can in fact make a big difference.

What has stopped you from taking action to be a Better Human in the past?

Something that has stopped me from taking action in the past was what I thought my peers would say about my fundraising. I was worried about what my friends would think, that no one would understand how important this was to me and that they wouldn't donate any money. Many teens assume things before even realizing what others want and I thought that some kids would think I was going to keep the money and that I wasn't going to make a difference. I think this has blocked me from taking action a few times in the past. I want to change in this way.

Tell me about a time when you failed trying to be a Better Human and what you did.

One time I failed being a Better Human was when I had a hard, long day at school. I was tired and grumpy, it was hard to be positive, and I didn't contribute to the family in a positive way. This didn't make me, or anyone feel good that day, and to be a Better Human I need to communicate better, to explain my feelings to those around me.

What's been your greatest challenge and how did you overcome that challenge to be a Better Human?

My greatest challenge to be a Better Human was to take the first step and overcome the fear of what might happen in my journey to raise money for my Poppa. At first I didn't know if my fundraising would be successful but I overcame this fear by just deciding to do it. I realized that I had the support of so many people and what I was doing for my Poppa was a good thing.

Is there something/someone that inspires you to be a Better Human? What is it that inspires you?

My Poppa inspires me to be a Better Human because every day he always has a smile on his face and he puts smiles on other peoples' faces too. He is able to talk to people and make everyone feel included and special. My Poppa has been supportive of me and always been by my side for whatever comes next and whatever challenges I face.

Has your life changed as a result of being a Better Human? Tell me how.

Being a Better Human has shaped my life today by feeling empathy towards others more often. I think about how my actions can affect others and how they make other people feel. I want my actions to make people feel better about themselves so they can spread their joy to other people. My Poppa changed my life too, he made me feel good to know that he believed in me along with my family. I started to understand that there are people out there who want to help and were very helpful with my fundraising efforts.

Tell me why young people can make a difference in the world if they take action.

Near the beginning of my fundraising I received an anonymous letter in the mail that contained a $50 donation towards my cause. The person thanked me for my hard work and creating awareness for my cause. This boosted my confidence knowing that complete strangers were supporting me during my journey. It showed me that people are willing to help young people, not just adults, and it made me realize that kids can make a difference.

Paul's Reflections

I think Owen's story touches us all. Our grandfathers, or Poppa as Owen says, are special people and having the mindfulness at such a young age to want to make a difference was heartwarming. Owen's honesty about what his friends would think about him raising money for his Poppa was real. His fear that "No one would understand how important this was to me" could have been a real barrier if he had let that stop him. Thankfully that wasn't the case and he was able to raise a considerable amount of money for prostate cancer research.

Seeing the Homeless

Katie is 16 years old and is in grade 11. She's a singer and guitar player and spends most of her days singing and hanging out with friends.

What does it mean to be a Better Human?

Being a Better Human means that you are kind and thoughtful to those around you and to those who aren't around you. I think you can be a good human to people you know as well as strangers. It includes picking up trash on the ground when I see it, wearing a mask during Covid when others are too embarrassed. I give homeless people money from my tips from busking downtown. It makes me sad to see those who are homeless and I want to help them.

Why is it important to you?

Being a Better Human is important to me because if one teen sets a good example of a Better Human then other teens will follow in their footsteps. We used to buy gifts and put them in shoe boxes and send them to children in other countries. I felt like these gift boxes would help make the homeless people's day just a little bit better. Perhaps others will notice me doing this and they will join in with me to do the same and more homeless will get care packages too. I'm trying to show others how they can make a difference too.

Tell me a story about a time when you did something to be a Better Human. What was the impact of that? How did it make you feel?

Last year at Christmas time I saved up some of my money and decided to create some care packages in a shoe box (Gloves, socks, water, granola bars, chapstick, and candy canes for Christmas) and hand them out to the homeless people. It was a very interesting experience and some people had lots of stories to tell. Their stories definitely changed my perspective on life. In the past I used to just think "That's sad" but now I see opportunities to help the homeless. I met a man who used to be married with four sons and now he's homeless and has no family. It makes me want to live life to the fullest and not back down on good opportunities and live life now.

What is something specific you want to do to be a Better Human?

I want to help others and continue to create care packages for homeless people because seeing them struggle makes me feel really bad and I want to help them. My goal is to make more care packages than last year and hand those out to the homeless. I also want to spend more time handing out the care packages and learn more about those that I give the care packages to and let them know that they're not alone. I'm hoping that by interacting with them it will help make their day better.

What advice would you give to other teens if they want to be Better Humans today?

The advice I would give to teens is to be more polite to others and make sure to do your part in the community. Volunteering at bottle drives, working at a soup kitchen all help, picking up garbage on the street, not vandalizing property in the neighbourhood. Finding the right friends who have the same mindset as me is important.

What has stopped you from taking action to be a Better Human in the past?

Something that has stopped me from being a Better Human in the past is being made fun of by other people when trying to do something kind. I haven't handed out my care packages with my friends because I was afraid that they would make fun of me and that they wouldn't see what I see.

Tell me about a time when you failed trying to be a Better Human and what you did.

My first year creating the packages for the homeless was harder than the others. It was my first experience doing it and I had packages left over. If I had spent a few more hours finding more people I would have been able to deliver them all. I didn't know how to determine who was homeless and who wasn't. I was also nervous because it was my first year and I assumed, based on what I had been told by others, that they just weren't good people, drug addicts and alcoholics. But, after speaking with them and getting to know their stories, my perspective about the homeless changed.

What's been your greatest challenge and how did you overcome that challenge to be a Better Human?

A couple years back when I was in middle school there was this girl who would always think she was better than everyone else. This made me really annoyed and she made me feel like I couldn't do anything without being criticized. It took some time for me to realize that if I turned the negative energy I used on her into positive energy for myself, I could focus more on my talents and be a better person to her.

One day I decided to change friends and focus more on what would make me happy. I started going to Open Mic events, and I tried to be nicer to her by giving her a solo performance in our Choir that I had been picked to perform.

Is there something/someone that inspires you to be a Better Human? What is it that inspires you?

My older brother Theron has inspired me so much to be a Better Human, he has incredible leadership skills and is kind to everyone around him. Theron and I both volunteer at Foster Parent events and he is so good with the kids and connects with them very easily. He's not afraid to do the things that he sets his mind to, he doesn't appear to be scared and that's inspiring. He's so patient with our younger siblings and I ask "How does he do that?" It makes me believe that I could be better and more patient.

Has your life changed as a result of being a Better Human? Tell me how.

I think that since I've begun being a Better Human I have been more sympathetic, empathetic, kind and patient to those around me. I see the homeless for the person that they are, rather than the person who I was told they were. I give money to them and see them now. I also see opportunities to help the homeless rather than simply walking by them.

I believe I definitely have more confidence, I'm not really afraid to sing in front of people and I want others to know that is what I love to do. I really believe that you have to go for it and do what you really love. Don't worry about what other people are going to think about you, and if you mess things up it's all part of the plan. I always mess up but that is how we learn.

Tell me why young people can make a difference in the world if they take action?

If teens decide that they want to be Better Humans, then other kids will want to do the same. They will grow up to be better influences for other kids by leading and mentoring. If I'm a better teenager my younger siblings will see that and this will encourage them to be better too.

Paul's Reflections

Katie is a great example of how just one teenager can make a big difference. What struck me about this conversation was the empathy that Katie shows for the homeless. Her willingness to share her tips from busking downtown, and actually "seeing" the homeless really hit home; how many of us simply walk by and pretend they're not there? I also was moved by her confidence to simply just make the gift boxes and go find the homeless people and give them out. That really shows her confidence and determination to make a difference; this is leadership at its finest.

Allow the Day to Guide Us

Adam is a teen living with Autism and Epilepsy. He is originally from Europe and was adopted into Canada. He loves doing outdoor adventures, sports, theatre and much more. He likes trying new things that he may have an interest in. He has always loved connecting with people of all ages and backgrounds. He loves to make people laugh, by entertaining them with comedy. It makes him happy when he sees others happy. He also has a soulful side, where he loves guiding people, showing them a different look on life and experiences, to think out of the box.

Adam was recognized by Community Living British Columbia (CLBC) for his exceptional contribution to supporting people with different abilities to lead good lives, have rich relationships, and choices in how they live, work, and play. In 2013, Adam travelled to Parry Sound, ON to lead a community education initiative with municipal leaders about wheelchair accessibility within the small town. Adam has also spoken to students at Camosun College with a classmate from his Youth Leadership class about inclusion in classrooms and about how teachers could support students with different abilities.

In 2015, Adam was one of five British Columbians to receive the Widening Our World (WOW) Award for his volunteer work with Power to Be Adventure, Best Buddies, Lifetime Networks, and Aids Vancouver Island. Adam continues to volunteer with

Power to Be Adventure, Best Buddies, Lifetime Networks, and has added Embrace Arts Foundation, Paddle for Health, and Human Nature Counselling. As a person living with Autism and Epilepsy, Adam is also dedicated to teaching others about Autism, Epilepsy and other different abilities.

What does it mean to be a Better Human?

To be a Better Human, the first lessons in life we learn as humans are respect and patience, to follow these key words of life. Respect, accept, acknowledge, value, listen and hear (listening and hearing are 2 separate things). Remembering that everybody has a story and in order to get along we have to accept each other and adapt to accept everyone.

Why is it important to be a Better Human?

It's important to be a Better Human, because we learn how to be a human *being*, not a human *doing*. We learn to care for others as well as ourselves, and to respect all that's around us, feel balanced, and live life.

Tell me a story about a time when you did something to be a Better Human. What was the impact of that? How did it make you feel? Did you have any challenges?

I have always loved to guide people through this journey we call life, to help guide other kids/youths/teens and even grown ups in the key words of life (Respect, accept, acknowledge, value, listen and hear).

It makes me feel good and happy when I have been able to help others feel more at ease with life through communication, to help remind them that we don't need to rush and that we can allow the day to guide us. I have started to limit my social media/technology time and have noticed a difference, a really good difference, and I hope to share that with many others, so they too can have that balance. There are many challenges I do face on a daily basis, because of both my Autism and Epilepsy. I often will get asked if I wish I never had Epilepsy. I always say no, actually I'm super thankful. Because of those experiences, it's helped me and allowed me to see the world in many different ways.

I had a near death experience in November, 2019. Thankfully I made it through, but because of that experience, it has allowed me to let the day guide me, to not rush through things just because the majority of others are. It showed to be more respectful about all that's around me; the simplicity of life, that it is ok to feel certain emotions, to know you have a right to be who you are as a person, a human being, how to learn from mistakes, how to accept and respect some challenges that we might end up facing one day. It taught me that all humans are different and that's what makes the human species incredible; we learn to adapt because of these challenges, and when we adapt, we become more accessible for all.

What is something specific you want to do to be a Better Human?

Something specific I would like to do to be a Better Human being is to be able to guide more people than just in my hometown. I would like to do a TED talk and give more presentations to a variety of organizations, including emergency services, about people with different abilities.

What advice would you give to teens if they want to be Better Humans today?

To know that we have mistakes for a reason, that we can use those mistakes as guidance instead of being labeled as a "bad kid" because of a choice we made, when maybe we shouldn't have. To know that there are challenges in life for a reason. Those challenges we have everyday are the ones that guide us into being a stronger human being. It allows growth of the human species, it allows humans to problem solve and much more.

Life is not meant to sound like "I just can't wait for the weekend, so I can enjoy my weekend, my little holiday I have" and hate the rest of the week. Every day of our life should matter, it should be fruitful, and have a purpose. We need to live, not just survive. We can all just put on a "fake mask" and act like "Yay, I'm so happy, but "fake masks" are the reason so many people are lost in this world. We can slow down, gather our thoughts, our passion, and purpose, to be who we are as a person first. We need a balance of fun and positives as well in our lives.

What's been your greatest challenge and how did you overcome that challenge to be a Better Human?

When I get into deep conversations with others, where I feel I need to change how I am trying to guide that one specific individual to learn and accept that there will be others out there who just "don't care." Instead of taking that as a type of "hate," I try to see that maybe they are just in a time and space where they are not ready, and that there are other ways to help guide others.

Another challenge I had was the death of a human being who I called my mum (foster). I didn't get many years with her when I was younger because she had passed away from cancer (multiple brain tumours). Not long after I had a few friends passed away due to medical conditions. Because of those challenging experiences of losing somebody so close, it also also taught me a lot about grief. I've learned to not fear grief, but to allow it to do what it needs to do, to respect the time it needs, to know that grief will be different for everyone, and that it is a healthy thing for humans. I've also learned about healthy fear vs "panic fear" especially right now with the Coronavirus. We need healthy fear because it protects us, but also allows us to grow, and problem solve and move forward; the "panic fear" is what stops us from being able to grow and move forward.

These challenges have guided me to know that we can live in the moment, that we can think about the past and future, but we don't need to rush, and we don't need to over focus.

Is there something/someone that inspires you to be a Better Human? What is it that inspires you?

The organizations that I call family (Power to Be, Human Nature Counselling, Embrace Arts Foundation) inspire me. Seeing the passion they have, the willingness they have, the want and the need to guide humans into human *beings* and to get out of that human *doing* state. To have our natural connections given back to the human species, nature, our home, the simplicity of life.

They inspire me because of the passion they have. I hope to continue their journey one day, so that many other teens now, and in future generations, can have the experience I've been so thankful for.

Has your life changed as a result of being a Better Human? Tell me how.

Incredibly, it's allowed me to meet so many people all around, with many different backgrounds. It's allowed me to not only listen to others, but to *hear* them, hear their story, because everyone has a voice, no matter what age. If one has a different ability, or has come from a different country, we are one, that's why I have changed to using "we" more often than "I" in certain conversations. Because a lot of things we do, we couldn't have done if it wasn't for the connection and the experiences of one another. We need each other, we need to support and care for each other.

It's also allowed me to accept and respect, acknowledge, value, even listen and hear different abilities, my own personal different abilities. I am proud to let others know I have Autism, I have epilepsy/seizures, even Asthma. I have learned so much about the human body because of all of those, how to properly take care of myself, and even others.

Tell me why young people can make a difference in the world if they take action.

Because too many times we get shut down because we are "just kids", we are teens, human beings, individuals. Life can only grow when we learn to hear everyone's voice. Age is only a number that was never natural to the human species. By putting age on to a human being, it not only keeps track of how long one has lived, but it also puts up a huge barrier, because it blocks voices out, it blocks the respect to listening and hearing others of all "ages."

Humans need to be able to listen and hear one another, because that's how humans grow, that's how we learn to do things, to problem solve. This is why it's also important to listen and hear what other countries do during global situations.

What has stopped you from taking action to be a Better Human in the past?

There have been moments where I felt like giving up, because I felt like my message, my voice, wasn't being heard by some people. I didn't like the clashing arguments we would end up with, I didn't like the feeling of being shut down when I tried to voice my personal opinion about something. It didn't make sense to me why they "had the right" but I didn't, even though we were both expressing personal opinions about the same topic. Sometimes it would make me want to avoid certain situations, but I've learned when we avoid, it doesn't solve anything. We need to problem solve so we don't have to avoid situations, and can move forward. I've always been the type who would try to figure out other options, other ways so I can continue what I am passionate about.

Tell me about a time when you failed trying to be a Better Human and what you did.

There have been many times. Sometimes it was because of how I would end up doing it, and it didn't end up being the "best way" as I thought it would be. Sometimes I would say or do something I didn't mean to do and it made me feel bad because it's not who I am as a person. I've learned about "choosing your battle"; to stop and think how it might be for that individual, how they might be processing things, to get a better understanding of them, so I can know how to connect with them better.

Paul's Reflections

This interview with Adam was filled with many words of wisdom. What's most impressive is the fact that Adam is only 16. He makes it clear that he is going to live a life full of "doing" rather than just "being." Despite his challenges with Autism and Epilepsy, Adam is clearly leading the way and showing people with different abilities how to thrive today. Adam's commitment to his family of charities shows just how much of a difference one teen can make.

Doing the Right Thing - Always!

Markez Cain is a 13 year old student who is an aspiring basketball player. He lives with his mom and brother and believes in doing what is right despite what others say and do. Markez is a natural leader, and regularly shows his friends how to be Better Humans. He is an artist who enjoys drawing, volunteering, and cooking at home. He is kind and compassionate, cares about the well being of others, and loves to make people laugh.

What does it mean to be a Better Human?

Being selfless and helping other people. Love on people, the world needs more people loving on others. As a family, we often help others who have less than us. We see the homeless and want to help them through giving them money or buying them food. My brother demonstrates to our family how important this is. I like to invite others to join me and my friends when it seems like they are there alone so that they don't feel isolated. I regularly volunteer at my school with various tasks.

Why is it important to you?

You should always treat people the way you want to be treated. I'm a fun guy! I like to see people happy and have fun. I believe in being a leader in my life and want to be a great example to my friends and teachers. I think it's important to demonstrate to my peers that we can do more to create a better environment for ourselves and our futures.

Tell me a story about a time when you did something to be a Better Human. What was the impact of that? How did it make you feel?

As an athlete I always like to play positions where I can include teammates. I always remember having this one teammate on my basketball team that was new to the game and afraid to shoot. I just kept passing to him and passing to him; he kept missing his shots and I could feel his confidence dwindling. After one of our time outs was over and we were going back onto the court I told him, "I'll keep getting the ball to you, just keep shooting." Finally, one of his shots fell and our whole team went crazy; I'll never forget the look on his face! My whole heart smiled for him that day because I knew inside that he could make the shot and I wanted him to believe in himself and feel that he was an important part of the team.

What is something specific you want to do to be a Better Human?

Give back to people who are less fortunate than I am. When I'm older I want to spend lots of time going back into the communities that have helped raise me and assist in creating a new generation of Better Humans. My dream is to join the NBA and help my family as well as organizations like the Boys & Girls Club, and to create more opportunities for kids by building outdoor community sports parks.

What advice would you give to other teens if they want to be Better Humans today?

I would say no good deed goes unnoticed! No matter how small an impact you think your gesture may have, do it anyway. Then overtime you'll be being referred to as a "Better Human" while just being yourself. I don't think teens should worry about what their friends say when doing the right thing. I think it's important to make a difference despite anyone judging you or making fun of you for doing it.

What has stopped you from taking action to be a Better Human in the past?

I'm not the type of person to really let anything stop me from doing what I believe is the right thing to do. I don't let criticism or being made fun of by others stop me either. If I believe that something is the right thing to do, I encourage my friends to join me and be part of the good deed by leading the way and being the example.

Tell me about a time when you failed trying to be a Better Human and what you did.

This is a tough one to answer. I have never really failed to do the right thing because it's been the way that I have always been. I don't have to "decide" anymore based on the circumstance at the time, instead, I consistently - and without hesitation - do what needs to be done to make a difference.

What's been your greatest challenge and how did you overcome that challenge to be a Better Human?

Having a single Mom. She's awesome and she works really hard to give my brother and I everything we need (and want) but I know it's hard for her and it's challenging for me to watch. I overcome this by trying to help her out as much as I can. I help clean up and complete any chores that she asks me to. That way it frees up time for my mom to have some alone time and relax.

Is there something/someone that inspires you to be a Better Human? What is it that inspires you?

My grandmother. What she does for me and for other people, I want to be like that. My Nan makes friends everywhere she goes, and everyone loves her; she makes everyone feel like they're part of our family. I like that.

Has your life changed as a result of being a Better Human? Tell me how.

My Mom always tells me I was just sort of born seeing the brighter side of life. I really think that I grew up in a home where my mom demonstrated on a daily basis how to be a Better Human. She was my first true role model; she has a big heart and always wanted the best for us kids. She realized how important it was to be a role model and wanted to show us just how to be a Better Human. I 100% believe that I have an advantage just because of the way that my mom raised my brother and me.

Tell me why young people can make a difference in the world if they take action.

We're the future! If I could get my peers on board to be like other good people our age, our society will keep getting better and better and then maybe, just maybe, we can end racism, inequality and discrimination. When you believe that you are doing something right you need tunnel vision and just do the task despite what you think other kids will say to you, or about you. If you lack the confidence to do the right thing I really encourage you to simply try and then feel how great it feels to put a smile on someone's face.

Paul's Reflections

This interview with Markez was a shining example of how a young man can be a leader every day. It also showed the value of having a great role model in his mom. Markez is mature beyond his years and how his mom described him, "Just sort of born seeing the brighter side of life," was clearly demonstrated in this interview. He has confidence and truly understands the need to lead his friends in the right direction. I interviewed Markez while his mom was sitting beside him and I could see just how proud she was of him. I can't wait to see Markez's name on the marquee.

How Volunteering Made Me a Leader

When Emily was a high school student, she loved to volunteer both in her school and her community. She organized several events in her school which included a book drive for a children's home in Peru and a hotdog fundraiser. In her community, she volunteered at the Intercultural Association as a homework buddy. Emily also helped children and fellow teenagers with their English and homework assignments since English was not their first language. Emily A. graduated highschool in 2014 and has a career in Early Childhood Development.

What does it mean to be a Better Human?

A Better Human is someone who strives to grow into a better version of themselves everyday. I think a Better Human is someone who is driven to go out into the world and change it for the better. They want everyone around them to feel included and confident in themselves and in their actions as a human being.

Why is it important to you?

Being a Better Human is important to me because I want to help the people around me be their best. This was shown through my actions of getting to know people in my school on a personal level and helping out wherever I could. When I do this I feel that I am making a difference in other people's lives which, in turn, helps me grow as a person.

Tell me a story about a time when you did something to be a Better Human. What was the impact of that? How did it make you feel?

In 2014, I was lucky enough to go to Peru to volunteer with Globe Aware at a children's home. This was a home for children to live in during the week to be able to go to school. I worked with children on their English and homework. I also built a Lorena Stove in a rural community which helped the family to be able to cook things safely. I was able to do something that was out of my comfort zone and see how being a Better Human impacts people. The impact for me personally was that I reflected on my life and realized how grateful I was for everything that I have. The children that I interacted with were able to receive one on one support from someone who wanted to see them succeed. Building the Lorena Stove allowed me to impact a family in a personal way. This made me feel that I was making a difference, to myself as a person, and the people around me. This resulted in me realizing that I wanted to work with children and make a positive difference in their lives; this experience in turn, led me to the current career that I have as an Early Childhood Educator.

What is something specific you want to do to be a Better Human?

My career goal to work with children and families in a supportive and caring manner became a reality as a result of my volunteering with Globe Aware. I felt that the best fit would be to work as an Early Childhood Educator in a daycare for lower income families. I wanted to feel that I was being a Better Human by making a difference in people's lives. Working with families that may need extra support is a way that I can feel good in the work that I am doing right now.

What advice would you give to other teens if they want to be Better Humans today?

My advice to other teenagers if they want to be a Better Human is to allow yourself to be open to growth and change. It may come as going out of your comfort zone and may seem scary but it is one of the greatest learning opportunities that can be achieved. I always volunteer at school, I helped my teacher as a teaching assistant, and I emceed the assemblies. At first I was terrified of public speaking, but after a while I got more used to it and gained confidence knowing that I could do it.

What has stopped you from taking action to be a Better Human in the past?

The biggest thing that has stopped me from being a Better Human in the past is being scared to speak up and put myself out there as a leader. I was a follower and I didn't see the need to put myself out there.

Tell me about a time when you failed trying to be a Better Human and what you did.

There was a time when we were playing California Kickball during gym class in grade 11. During the game there was a person who was not able to kick the ball as well as others on their team. Her teammates started to comment rudely whenever they kicked the ball. I noticed that this was happening and instead of saying something, I stood by and watched. After the class ended I made sure she was okay and reassured her that the comments from the kids were rude. On reflection I wish that I had said something at the time, but I was unsure of how to proceed in the moment.

What's been your greatest challenge and how did you overcome that challenge to be a Better Human?

My biggest challenge has been achieving academic success. I have always struggled in school and have had to overcome a lot of obstacles to get to where I am today. I overcame these obstacles by being determined and working hard. Luckily I always had great teachers and great parents who were always supportive and I would often reach out to them for help.

Is there something/someone that inspires you to be a Better Human? What is it that inspires you?

The person who inspires me to be a Better Human is Malala Yousafzai. She isn't afraid to fight for what she believes in and she never backs down from a challenge, even when it gets hard. This is the kind of mentality that I strive to have.

Has your life changed as a result of being a Better Human? Tell me how.

My life has changed as a result of being a Better Human in the sense that I have become more confident in myself. Searching for and experiencing new things has allowed me to grow and discover traits that I never knew I had. This has allowed me to broaden my goals in life because I have a clear idea of what I want to do.

Tell me why young people can make a difference in the world if they take action.

Young people can make a difference because we are the voice of the future and we can make our mark on the world by starting young and standing up for what we believe in. I learned that to get people to listen to you, you have to take chances and take the initiative to help nurture your passion. I've learned to be the first person to help others and how volunteering in my community helps those that need it most. I gained a lot of experience through volunteering and meeting a variety of people from the numerous agencies that I helped. This helped me develop my leadership skills and it definitely changed my perspective.

Paul's Reflections

What I found most interesting in talking with Emily was the confidence and experience that she gained from the simple act of volunteering. It really helped her to see more of the world and see how fortunate she was here at home and how little others had. As well, it really helped her to decide on what she wanted to do as a career. She used the term "leader" a lot in our conversation and how volunteering helped to develop that strength in her.

Stories compiled
by Hillary Rideout

Failure is not an Option

Ali Ahmad is a 16 year old spreading joy to our most vulnerable citizens during a time of need across the globe. His goals are ambitious and he might just accomplish them.

What does it mean to be a Better Human?

To me, being a Better Human means having a positive impact on your surroundings. Our ultimate goal should be to make the world better, or at least have a positive impact on the people around us. Empathy is the key. When we are too involved in ourselves, we don't see what is going on around us. Understanding what others are experiencing is important. Leadership is critical too - taking initiative and action, and being creative in coming up with effective solutions.

Why is it important to you?

I acknowledge that the future of this world is us, the younger generations. Therefore, I take it upon myself to make the people around me better, to think of solutions for problems the world is experiencing and to respect elders, as is our tradition.

Tell me a story about a time when you did something to be a Better Human. What was the impact of that? How did it make you feel?

I am part of the team that started the Joy4All organization (joy4all.ca), which strives to bring happiness to people's lives and connect youth with elders. Joy4All started in response to Covid-19, recognizing there were people who were especially vulnerable to social isolation. We started targeting the elderly, creating joyful messages and keeping them busy and happy, so their mental health was protected.

I am very proud to be a part of Joy4All, as I know that everyone who connects with us receives happiness. The responses we get from the elderly are especially motivating, as it confirms that we are helping them through this tough time.

I am responsible for communication, branding and external relations, as well as finding and recording content. The entire project is run by youth. It's powerful because we're empowering youth to make a difference. The younger generation is consumed by materialistic things like video games, television, etc., and we give them an opportunity to connect with others.

What is something specific you want to do to be a Better Human?

I want to help the most vulnerable and marginalized communities, as I know how much talent they have and I acknowledge that they do not deserve to be living the way they do.

I want to eliminate racism. There is no place for it in this world, no matter who we are, how we live, or what our skin color is. Racism is not a just action. We were all created the same. We are all human. I want to understand why people feel the need to be racist. Then I can think about how it can be solved.

What advice would you give to other teens if they want to be Better Humans today?

Please don't waste the chances given to you! The biggest thing I have noticed in the people around me is procrastination. The possibilities of what they can do and achieve are endless. They can solve major problems in the world, but they chose not to. This is not the time to be lazy. It is the time to make a difference in this world.

What has stopped you from taking action to be a Better Human in the past?

Doubt and fear. These are the only barriers to our goals. The doubt of failing and the fear of not being good enough is what has halted my progress in being a Better Human. However, I have acknowledged my weaknesses and I know how to deal with them.

Failure is the best teacher. I know what it feels like to fail, to lose. I also know how it feels to win and succeed. In soccer, I felt down when I failed, but I was so happy when I succeeded. I was never in a position to feel better than others when we won because I had experienced losing and I empathized with them. I'm not afraid to fail; it's inevitable. Instead of being scared of it, I accept and learn from it.

Overcoming the fear of not being good enough is critical to progress. You don't need to worry about what others think of you; you just have to be good enough for yourself. You can value others' points of view, but you don't have to let it make you feel worthless.

Tell me about a time when you failed trying to be a Better Human and what you did.

Doing something caring for someone else is never a failure to me.

What has been your greatest challenge and how did you overcome that challenge to be a Better Human?

Empathizing with others is one of the most difficult things to accomplish while trying to be a Better Human. But, once you can understand how someone else experiences a situation, it is so much easier to identify and solve the problems they are experiencing.

Is there something/someone that inspires you to be a Better Human? What is it that inspires you?

My goals of making people know they are not alone in this world, eliminating poverty, and giving everyone an equal chance of improving themselves and their lifestyles is what inspires me.

If you can understand what others are going through, you can help. Most people don't understand what poverty is like, and how hard people work to get out of it. The poor are neglected and don't get opportunities to better themselves. Everyone should have that opportunity.

I started feeling strongly about helping people in poverty when, in a social studies class, I learned how people have historically been treated unfairly. I made a connection to how people are now. The rich are getting richer and the poor are getting poorer. With decreasing consumerism from the middle class, the economy will fail if this continues.

Has your life changed as a result of being a Better Human? Tell me how.

Definitely. Since starting Joy4All, helping others has become second nature and I do it every chance I get. I look for opportunities to make the world better instead of waiting for the chances to come.

Doing this work has changed my mindset. I wasn't looking to make that big of a difference but now that I'm part of something that matters, it feels great. I want to keep feeling that way. That's why I keep looking for opportunities to make the world better. Before, I had ideas and I wanted to make a difference, but I didn't know what to do. Now I know that I can make a difference and I know how.

Tell me why young people can make a difference in the world if they take action.

Young people have the most amazing imaginations and determination. I believe that if they take action, many of the world's problems will be solved and the world will advance faster. Young people have incredible compassion. They have the power to solve many of the world's social problems.

Many people don't take action because they think they are alone. But, there are millions of people like us and if we can create an opportunity for everyone to come together, it would be so powerful.

Youth have the best opportunity to make a difference because we have the time and imagination to work on a problem. But we don't often get an opportunity. If we teach kids problem solving earlier and give them opportunities, they would learn that they can do anything.

I see it all as a loop; first you need to identify a problem, then you need to empathize with those affected by the problem, then you have to be creative enough to come up with an effective solution.

Hillary's Reflections

Ali was my first interview and he planted a strong seed in my brain; something that really struck me and stuck with me throughout my other interviews and in writing the rest of this book. Ali helped me understand the concept of empathy and how it plays a huge part in being able to truly help another person in the way they want or need to be helped.

Ali was also the one to suggest that adults can do more in creating opportunities for young people to get involved in their community or their "cause." On the plus side, young people tend to have more time and fewer responsibilities than adults. But they also often lack the ideas and courage to get involved; sometimes they don't know where or how to start.

So, as Ali suggests, perhaps if parents, schools, sports teams, volunteer organizations and other adult-driven groups create opportunities for young people to get involved - make it easy and accessible for them to do so - we'll see more teens getting involved earlier.

And how big are this teen's goals?! Ending racism and poverty are among what Ali hopes to accomplish in his lifetime. He's planning for his role in it right now! If that's not inspiring, I don't know what is.

Hoops, Hard Work and Happiness

MacLean M is a 13 year old basketball player, working everyday to achieve his goals and spread happiness along the way.

What does it mean to be a Better Human?

I think it means to help others and to be kind so that people know you're a trustworthy person that they can rely on. It means being real and not fake. Be yourself. I would describe it as being kind, considerate, and caring.

Why is it important to you?

It's an amazing feeling to know when I've done a kind thing for another person. It makes me feel better and them feel better. I like it when someone shares back with me that they are happy or appreciate my ways. It doesn't always come back from others but I am learning to deal with that.

Tell me a story about a time when you did something to be a Better Human. What was the impact of that? How did it make you feel?

One day, my brother and I were playing basketball on the driveway and the man across the street came out of the house and said something was not right and that he needed help.

He collapsed to the ground. I was really scared. He laid on his driveway, sweating so much, but he couldn't communicate with us. We didn't know what to do. My brother ran inside to grab a phone to call the police while I went trying to find people to help us. We got 2 people to help, who splashed water on him to cool him off.

It took the ambulance a while to come. They thought it was a prank call. Eventually, an ambulance arrived and took him to the hospital. It turns out he was having a stroke. He is doing amazing now; he can read and write again. We are closer now to the man and his family. He and his wife nominated my brother and me for an award from Alberta Health for helping out.

I was so happy with how it turned out. I was so relieved when I found out he was okay. It was so shocking to me; that I was just playing basketball and it happened and we saved his life. This experience gives me confidence that I can be better, and not be scared to try.

What is something specific you want to do to be a Better Human?

I always want to make others happy and feel included whenever I can. My basketball coach recently brought in a new kid. He was really quiet. I want to try and talk to him and get him to be comfortable with the team. And I want to have healthy relationships with other people. That means being good, nice and always kind to each other.

What advice would you give to other teens if they want to be Better Humans today?

Be the kindest and most caring person you can be. It's so easy to be rude, but always make sure you're being kind. Don't be defensive, especially when people you trust and love share their thoughts - even critical ones. Listen to what they say.

What has stopped you from taking action to be a Better Human in the past?

When people are mean it doesn't really make you want to be nice back. I don't start anything, but I don't go out of my way for them. I ignore them. I am not nervous about helping others; if I see a kid alone, I can understand what they're going through and will go up to them because I would hate to be the new kid and alone.

Tell me about a time when you failed trying to be a Better Human and what you did.

There was a time when I'd get an "attitude" during basketball games, when the referees weren't calling what I thought were fouls, or my teammates weren't following our plays. I didn't lead the team, I didn't listen to the coach, I didn't play my best. I would end up mentally checking out of the game. My parents would tell me that they could see how my mood was affecting my game. I thought about it and tried to fix it. Eventually, I could recognize when I was mad. I realized that my playing did get worse. So, I would choose to brush it off. I knew that only I could choose my attitude; not the refs, not my coaches, not my teammates. Now, if a teammate messes up, I help them. Now I listen to my coaches.

What has been your greatest challenge and how did you overcome that challenge to be a Better Human?

In one of my classes in grade 7, I felt like my teacher and I didn't have a positive relationship. The teacher seemed to judge me extra hard, and wasn't friendly with me like she was with other students. I always thought I did well. I worked hard and studied, and I got pretty good marks in that class. At the end of the day, I learned that I didn't need to have that teacher approve of me, and that I should still do my best in the class so that I could feel good about doing my best. When I feel I do my best, then the judgment from others is less important because I know myself and my effort.

Is there something/someone that inspires you to be a Better Human? What is it that inspires you?

I have a lot of people in my corner who push me and motivate me to be better. My family, friends, coaches, and trainers inspire me. My coaches at Genesis Basketball (genesisbasketball.net) are all great leaders; they teach us more than just basketball. They also teach us about being good people and about the four things we can control in life: body language, effort, attitude, and communication. We use that while playing ball, but also in life.

One of my coaches tells me that only 1% of athletes make it to division one of post secondary teams so if I want to make it there (and I do), then I need to work as hard as I can. He says: "If it's meant to be, it's up to me."

My mom and dad always support and challenge me, and help me surround myself with great friends and trainers. When I'm tired, they urge me to keep going and remind me of my goals of being a professional player.

I have also had some amazing teachers over the years. Teachers who have helped shape me into the person I am. I am still in contact with the special ones, even from elementary school.

Has your life changed as a result of being a Better Human? Tell me how.

I don't know that my life has changed, I feel like I'm just being me.

Tell me why young people can make a difference in the world if they take action.

Little things can go a long way. It's not about making big changes to have an impact. I can lead by example among my friends and teammates and they can show me too. Then together, we make each other better. If it starts local like that, it can build up and grow from there. If a person in my class is having trouble with something, I can help them out, and they might help me out later. Or helping someone carry their groceries might encourage them to do something nice for someone else that day. Small things like this help everyone.

Hillary's Reflections

MacLean was referred to me by a trusted friend because upon hearing about the type of teen I was looking to talk to, MacLean clearly fit the bill. MacLean is a wonderful example of someone who is committed to making his life mean something.

One of the things MacLean told me that had the biggest impact on me was when he reached out to the new kid on his basketball team. He recognized that his new teammates didn't know anyone, empathized that he was probably nervous about it, and went out of his way to make him feel not so alone. This is the kind of human I hope I am raising in my own home. I know what it's like to walk into a room and not recognize a soul; I think we all do. This seemingly simple act of MacLean saying "Hi" and asking a few questions, or inviting him to join the group, probably felt to this kid like someone swooped in, picked him up, and made him believe everything was going to be okay. It was a simple act that had a huge impact.

While I call what MacLean did a "simple act," it's not lost on me that what he did took courage. The other boy could have acted badly; could have rejected MacLean, but he chose to not let that risk stop him. To me, that's what it means to be a Better Human. At the age of 13, MacLean gets it.

Dog's Best Friend

Nick is a 16 year old who, since the age of 8, has turned his love for animals into life saving missions.

What does it mean to be a Better Human?

My definition of being a Better Human means that you are willing to do things for the betterment of others over yourself. It's about self-sacrifice and a willingness to help others.

Why is it important to you?

Being a Better Human is important to me because it makes me feel happy about the fact that I help people and animals. It all gives me a sense of pride. The animals I help get to leave the bad place they are in and get a new loving home. If we don't help them, they may get killed. There's also an impact on the families who foster and adopt the dogs. It gives them an opportunity to adopt a dog in need and give it a loving family and home.

Tell me a story about a time when you did something to be a Better Human. What was the impact of that? How did it make you feel?

My family does a lot of work with BARCs Rescue (barcsrescue. com). It is a no-kill organization that rescues dogs who are on death row at high kill shelters in the US and Canada, with the ultimate goal of placing them in loving, permanent homes. We try our best to help as many dogs as we can. We locate the dogs, transport them, seek out foster and adoptive families, and raise donations to support the dogs once they are in our care. Recognizing that every dog deserves a chance, BARCs does not discriminate on the basis of age, health or breed. We dedicate every resource at our disposal to the physical, emotional and behavioral rehabilitation of each animal that we rescue.

I started with BARCs when I was 8 years old. I would set up and break down kennels for the rescued dogs. Over time, my responsibilities increased to be more involved with the animals. I help out by taking rescued dogs out of their kennels to the veterinary doctor, and then introducing them to their foster families.

The first time I got to help actually retrieve a group of dogs was when I went on a transport mission to Saskatoon. That transport had a very large impact because we brought back 55 dogs. There was one dog named Nike who, according to the people living on the reserve where we found him, was a "trouble" dog who was aggressive toward people. We got him and put him in a kennel on the bus. During the drive back, I would walk back towards his kennel every so often and just sit there petting him, giving him food and company. During the whole ride, he just sat there and enjoyed my company. He was never a "bad" dog; it must have been the way he was treated that caused him to lash out and act in an aggressive manner. Now he is living in a new home and is enjoying life. He is able to be the sweet dog I know and love. He is actually a bit of a hero in that he scared off a bear while his new owner was taking out the garbage!

This transport made me feel an overwhelming sense of joy because I had helped save these 55 dogs from a very negative life, and got them into new and loving homes.

I got involved with BARCs when I was 8 years old. My family was looking to get a new dog and we discovered BARCs and started to foster dogs. Our very first foster dog would constantly poop as he walked through the house and we figured that if that didn't scare us off, we were meant to foster more! My parents and I started helping out with BARCs work. Now we're involved all the time.

What is something specific you want to do to be a Better Human?

I want to be able to continue to help both humans and animals. Ultimately, I want all animals to have loving homes away from abusive houses or deadly situations. I will keep working with BARCs; it makes me feel like a better person. I want to keep rescuing the dogs and giving them to loving families; helping out with everything. I find it fun!

My family also volunteers to help feed the hungry. We prepare food and make lunch bags for the homeless. I want to continue helping those who don't have the best possible life; I want to make their day a little better.

What advice would you give to other teens if they want to be Better Humans today?

Just go out and get yourself out there. Try new things and try to make a difference, even if it's a small difference. Every little bit counts.

What has stopped you from taking action to be a Better Human in the past?

Anxiety, stress, and not being old enough to be able to do certain things. I have pretty bad anxiety; I don't like to be around new people. It has stopped me. I do sometimes push through it, but sometimes it stops me in my tracks. I find it too stressful and I'll stop, even when I know I could do something to help someone.

Tell me about a time when you failed trying to be a Better Human and what you did.

When I get too focused playing video games, it takes me away from the world into my own zone where I don't pay attention to anything going on around me. Gaming changes me. The reason I play them is because they help me get rid of anxiety. I can play for hours and hours a day, non-stop, in hopes of getting rid of some of the anxiety. It works sometimes, but not always. When I get too focused on playing, I can get stubborn or rude and I don't help around the house as much because I don't see what's going on around me.

What's been your greatest challenge and how did you overcome that challenge to be a Better Human?

Anxiety has been my greatest challenge. It holds me back from being my full self when I'm not with people I know. It makes me feel that if I mess up, everyone will judge me. It feels as though I want to say or do something but I physically can't; it can be frightening. The only way I know how to overcome it is to take a deep breath and think of something else, to continually push myself out of my comfort zone.

Is there something/someone that inspires you to be a Better Human? What is it that inspires you?

My parents; they are always there for everyone. Even if someone is rude to them, they will push that to the side to be able to help them. They've always been there for me. They would do anything for me, to help me. They'll help anyone. One time, I saw my dad give CPR to someone who had passed out. He saved his life. My mom and dad always give 110%. They inspire me to do my best all the time.

Has your life changed as a result of being a Better Human? Tell me how.

I feel like I have accomplished more than if I had just been my normal self. I feel like I have actually contributed to the world in a helpful way. I don't just sit around. I go out and try to help others instead of just looking out for myself. Being a Better Human is about turning your thoughts into action. It's just something that is naturally in me.

Tell me why young people can make a difference in the world if they take action.

Young people can make a difference because every small act they do will add up to something bigger over time. If they get out there and try to help with something, from volunteering at an old folks home to helping to feed the hungry or helping someone cross the street or giving a meal to someone who can't afford to eat...these small things will add up overtime and make the world a better place. I want a world where every person is happy, living in a nice home, and no one is worrying about their next meal. One act of kindness carries on to others and they'll spread it. One act of kindness might be small but it's going to change how people think, and that's powerful.

Hillary's Reflections

Nick is someone I sought out to interview. I am a HUGE animal lover and it was very important to me that we include an interview with someone who is focused on helping animals. Barcs Rescue helps the most vulnerable dogs - those who others don't have the resources to help. What Nick and his team do is nothing short of life saving.

Nick's parents have had a lot to do with his involvement in dog rescue. They have given him opportunities and he is following their cues. It's not surprising, but worth mentioning, that parents can have incredible influence on their children. Nick's parents lead by example and he is open to following that lead.

I was really touched by Nick's openness and willingness to share his experiences with anxiety and fear of others' judgement. Many of us have anxiety about this and different things. Nick found this prevented him from doing things he wanted to. He hasn't found a magic solution, but he has learned that if he can notice his anxious feelings, take a few deep breaths, and make a conscious decision to move through the feelings, he can come out the other side. And when he does this, he can be his true Better Human self. What a brave thing.

Snowballs and Avalanches

Finley Foster is 13. At the age of 10...TEN...gathered a group of friends and led them to lives of giving back to their community. He is a true leader.

What does it mean to be a Better Human?

It means to spend your life helping others.

Why is it important to you?

Because I don't want to live my life without having done good on this earth. I want to help people before I die. I don't want to be forgotten. I want to be remembered for someone who has done something to help others.

Tell me a story about a time when you did something to be a Better Human. What was the impact of that? How did it make you feel?

In fifth grade, I had an assignment in class. It was to create a "passion project." We could do anything. I had read a book earlier that year about a kid who started a club and I wanted to do the same. I sent out texts to all my friends and invited them to a meeting in the park. I told them about my idea to come together to do humanitarian things for others. To my surprise, most of them showed up! We call it the Positive Action Group, or PAG. We started by doing something once or twice a month. It's as simple as that!

Now, at the beginning of each year, we send out a sign up list so members can sign up to lead an activity in the month they choose. Each volunteer leader comes up with the activity and completely plans it. Then, the other members are asked to show up and help.

What inspired me was a book we read as a class in grade 5. It was about a kid who was addicted to video games (much like me). His parents didn't like it. They wanted him to do more *real* stuff (much like me). One day, the kid's house almost burned down because he was playing video games and hadn't noticed a fire. After that, he was grounded until he did something at school, like get better grades or join or start a club. He created the Positive Action Group...it was actually a lie to make his parents think he was doing something good. But, he had to put on the school website, so everyone saw it. And kids actually wanted to join so he actually had to do it!

After starting our PAG, one of the activities we did that was extra fulfilling for me was to volunteer at a place that serves homeless people. It's called Love and Light Ministries. We donated supplies and helped them package necessities for homeless people. The impact of knowing a homeless person's life was going to be made just a little better made me feel happy and fulfilled. Also, the lady who began Love and Light Ministries used to be homeless herself as a teenager, so it made us feel like she really knew what homeless people needed most.

What is something specific you want to do to be a Better Human?

I'm not sure about something "specific." I'm very open to ideas of how to help others. But I would like to grow PAG to include many more people and to have a wider impact, maybe even when we are adults.

What advice would you give to other teens if they want to be Better Humans today?

Just be brave and do SOMETHING, no matter how small. It's those first small steps that can snowball into avalanches of impact. We are never too young to make a difference.

What has stopped you from taking action to be a Better Human in the past?

Feeling like I don't fit in. Sometimes there are groups that I could join, or activities that I could do that would be good and helpful, but because I'm not part of the group, I can't work up the courage to join. I don't like to join a group after they've already started. I've somewhat overcome it but sometimes I still get nervous.

Tell me about a time when you failed trying to be a Better Human and what you did.

I have failed at many things many times in my life, but I honestly can't remember a time when I have failed when I have actually

TRIED to be a Better Human. It's almost as if the trying alone makes you a Better Human.

What's been your greatest challenge and how did you overcome that challenge to be a Better Human?

One of our biggest challenges with PAG was when we tried to give a bike to a homeless man who we had helped on other occasions and had tried to befriend. We went to a local bike shop owner and talked to him about the homeless man. It turned out that he had actually tried to help the same man in the past. We tracked the homeless man down and tried to explain to him how we thought the bike would help him and told him where he could meet us to get the bike, but he was very unsure about it. He told us he didn't know how to ride a bike, and we told him the bike owner had offered to teach him on the bike shop property. Unfortunately, he never showed up to get the bike.

That was a disappointment for sure, but we learned a lot about homelessness through that experience. One of those things was that what we think are the best ways to help others aren't necessarily what they really need. It helped us learn to try to walk in others' shoes to try to figure out what others *really* need. I think the way we overcame this challenge was to realize that not every endeavor we undertake is necessarily going to be successful, but not to give up, and instead, learn what we can from the experience and move forward.

Is there something/someone that inspires you to be a Better Human? What is it that inspires you?

The author of the book I mentioned inspired me to become a better person and start a real-life group to help others. After reading his book, I just felt that I hadn't done enough to help others. Even now I want to do more. I want the group to continue, hopefully into my adulthood. I feel like I've accomplished a lot, but not enough.

Has your life changed as a result of being a Better Human? Tell me how.

I feel better about myself, but I don't necessarily feel like my life has changed that much. I feel fulfilled, refreshed, and human. It makes me feel really good. I never thought a kid at my age could do something so big. To have such a big impact at such a young age, I am very proud of myself and the group.

Tell me why young people can make a difference in the world if they take action.

Because we have just as much power as adults to do good things. If we put our minds to it, we can do just as much as an adult. We just need to speak up and for people to listen to us.

Hillary's Reflections

I can't glaze over the fact that Finley was TEN when he started the Positive Action Group. It's truly remarkable that he believed he could make a difference at such a young age. There had to be something innate inside of him, like he was destined to do wonderful things and he had the confidence it took. He also recognized inspiration when he saw it, and had the incredible support of his family and friends who were willing to follow his lead.

Finley has been a true leader in how he has challenged others to take accountability for leading activities that they are passionate about. This is where the real magic comes... Finley has made countless other kids feel like they can make a difference. In his own words: "We are never too young to make a difference."

Something else Finley said to me was that although he's experienced challenges in his Better Human work, he hasn't experienced failure. He believes that as long as you're trying, you *are* being a Better Human.

Making Ripples Turn into Waves

Mason C is a 13 year old who refuses to allow disease to stop him from spreading positivity.

What does it mean to be a Better Human?

It's important to send a positive ripple out into the world. One negative ripple can sometimes be more powerful than a positive ripple, which affects everyone. There are always going to be things you don't like, so if you can try to find a silver lining, things are easier to get through. People are more likely to be positive if you're positive. It kind of creates a contagious atmosphere. One negative person can bring everyone down, but one positive person can turn everyone around. Basically, if you can make yourself your *best* self, or like you call it, a Better Human, then you send out a positive ripple to everyone else that helps them do the same and be their best selves too.

Why is it important to you?

At the end of the day, I feel better about myself when I've done something nice for someone else or helped someone. It makes me feel proud and fulfilled.

Tell me a story about a time when you did something to be a Better Human. What was the impact of that? How did it make you feel?

I'm a member of a group called the Positive Action Group (PAG) at school. Every month we get together and do an activity or visit an organization and help where we are needed. One month, when it was my turn to organize an event, we put together supply packs for the homeless. Everyone came over to my house with items from a list I created so that we could make a bunch of packs filled with items we thought people needed. We included things like toothbrushes, toothpaste, water bottles, snacks, socks, gloves and some other things. We all kept multiple packs in our parents' cars, so that when we were driving by someone who was homeless at a street light, we could hand them out.

Handing out the packs made me feel really good. There was one guy who took the bag from my dad when he handed it out the window and he was so excited. He said, "Oh WOW! There's even gloves in here!!! Thanks man, this is awesome!" Seeing his reaction made me want to do more good things.

What is something specific you want to do to be a Better Human?

I would like to write a book for kids about what it's like to be sick, with strategies you can use and things you can do to get better. About a year ago, I got really sick and I wasn't able to do much. I spent months seeing different doctors and specialists who gave me a lot of different advice. Some of the advice was really good, but it didn't really start to help me until we found a way to put it all together in a way that worked for me. There is a lot of information out there for parents, but not a lot that is specifically for kids. If there had been something like this around when I got sick, it would have been really helpful.

What advice would you give to other teens if they want to be Better Humans today?

Always stay positive. If you want to do something big, that's great! Go for it! But, you don't always have to do something big. Every wave starts out small. The little ripples can be enough to make really big changes in the world. You don't have to be the organizer or the creator of some big thing. If you see someone else out there trying to be a Better Human, you can join their endeavor. If you don't have your own idea, it's great to help someone else if you believe in what they are doing.

What has stopped you from taking action to be a Better Human in the past?

Before I joined the PAG I didn't have an idea of how I could help or even, as a kid, if I could have an impact. But after we started our monthly projects, it showed me that I could make a difference and really help people.

Tell me about a time when you failed trying to be a Better Human and what you did.

I don't think you can fail when you try to be a Better Human. If you put in your best effort, then you are still making a positive difference and can know at the end of the day that you did the right thing.

What's been your greatest challenge and how did you overcome that challenge to be a Better Human?

When I got sick, everything became a challenge. I was tired, I hurt a lot and I didn't have enough energy to do much. I wasn't able to go to school or see my friends and I missed out on a lot. It was a lot to deal with, but I was really glad I got to take trips around the country to see so many doctors. I tried to make the best of it and focus more on what was good to help me get through it, like the amazing places I visited and things I saw.

Our family had lots of time together and I especially loved the one-on-one time I had with my mom; when I felt awful, we would sit and read together. Those were really special bonding times. As hard as it was, there were lots of moments that were full of smiles. I even got to jump the line at the airport! I tried to make my own positive ripples and I never lost hope. I trusted that things would get better. Something that my mom has helped me understand is that everything is temporary; both the highs and the lows. Everything changes. So when things seem dark, I know that the light will come again.

Is there something/someone that inspires you to be a Better Human? What is it that inspires you?

I don't know if there is a specific inspiration. I just like to know at the end of the day that I helped someone. It makes me feel good.

Has your life changed as a result of being a Better Human? Tell me how.

I get to be around other people who want to do good things in the world together and it amplifies the effect. It's fun and I feel good about it.

Tell me why young people can make a difference in the world if they take action.

We have a lot of time left in the world and if we start now, we can have more of an effect than if we wait until we are adults. Create or join a group that goes around helping people or just simply be a good person. Be positive, say nice things and have a good attitude. The world needs more people who are kind, help each other and support each other. Putting yourself in other people's shoes to understand how they feel helps you better understand how to help them.

Hillary's Reflections

At 13, Mason is one of the most positive, optimistic people I've met. He is quiet and humble; his shyness is endearing. And wow, he is strong! Learning of his medical challenges and hearing that he found happiness in the quietest, sweetest, simplest moments is truly inspiring. Somehow he's been able to hold onto hope and trust that things will be better. He knows his optimism has everything to do with making better days a reality. We could all learn something from Mason - that there is always a silver lining and resilience is built from recognizing the good in even the toughest circumstances.

Mason plans to create resources for kids who find themselves in similar situations to him, to provide them with insight and support designed especially for them and I believe he will accomplish these goals and help many people.

Recruited by a Tick

Olivia Goodreau developed Lyme disease from a tick bite when she was 6. Now she's 16 and the founder of a foundation that is helping other young people live with the debilitating effects of the disease. She believes she was "recruited by a tick" to help others. Wow.

What does it mean to be a Better Human?

To be a Better Human means to have empathy for others. It means listening to their concerns and being open to help, whether you know them or not. You have to be dedicated and able to work with others to achieve goals. You should never think you can't do something, because that doubt will get in the way. If you want to see a change, change it.

Why is it important to you?

It has always been a part of who I am. I want to help others because I would want someone to help me if I were in a tough situation. I want to be the person I needed all those years ago.

During the summer between my first and second grades - I was 6 years old - at a lake in Missouri, I was bitten by a tick outside of my house. I didn't know it had happened; I hadn't felt it and I didn't have a rash. A few weeks went by and I couldn't lift my head, I had a tremor in my right hand, and I started having blackouts. It felt like a flu that wouldn't go away.

Over the next 18 months I saw 51 doctors. I had multiple MRIs, CT scans, EKGs, spinal taps, EEGs, a liver biopsy, upper and lower endoscopy, over 100 blood draws, and I had my adenoids removed.

It wasn't until we saw the 51st doctor that I was diagnosed with Lyme disease. I was put on a 30 day treatment and was told that I'd be back to normal. Unfortunately, after that treatment was over, I was not back to normal. Over the next 3 years and more doctors, I was diagnosed with several other conditions in addition to Lyme. It took the 54th doctor to discover what 53 others had missed.

While learning to manage my health conditions I heard a story about a little boy and his mother who were living in their car because they had sold everything to pay for his Lyme disease medication. That story stuck with me and I knew that I couldn't sit and wait for someone else to make a change. *I* had to do it. In January 2017, I developed the LivLyme Foundation (livlymefoundation.org). The Foundation raises money for families who cannot afford medication for their children, as well as to fund research and search for a cure for all of us suffering from tick borne illnesses.

Tell me a story about a time when you did something to be a Better Human. What was the impact of that? How did it make you feel?

A little girl who also had Lyme disease wanted to talk to me on the phone, to share her story with me. We talked for an hour, her telling me about herself and asking me questions, and me listening and helping her find answers. After the talk, I realized that I had become the person I had needed when I was younger. I would have loved it if someone had listened to me and helped me when I was in the hospital, seeing over 50 doctors who couldn't figure out what was wrong. This one conversation made me feel so happy and proud of how far I had come.

What is something specific you want to do to be a Better Human?

I want to travel around the world to meet people who share both the same and different causes that I do. I want to help as many people as possible, whether it's to visit a new scientist's lab to see what they're doing to help tick borne illnesses and determine which labs our Foundation will provide grants, or helping kids in their homes - spending time with them, like a big sister who has been where they are and to make their day less painful. I want to do talks at the schools/camps/churches of kids with Lyme disease, to help educate others and spread the message. That's something that would have helped me because people didn't understand why I was the way I was.

I want to see what other countries are doing; widen my horizons. I want to help everyone, even outside of the US. I want to help kids around the world.

What advice would you give to other teens if they want to be Better Humans today?

To be a Better Human, you must see everyone as equal and be willing to help anyone. You must try to help anyone in need.

My issue was a very personal one. You've got to find something you really care about; something you can envision being invested in for the long run. It's not about doing one fundraiser and you're done. One fundraiser can start it, but think bigger. Make sure you're invested in it and it's what you want to do. Then commit to it and go for it.

When starting a foundation, you have to go all in. You have to think about where you want to be in 4 or 5 years, and make a plan. Talk to people who are involved in the issue you care about; learn from them to understand what they've experienced. Volunteer at a foundation to learn how it works. Surround yourself with people who care about it as much as you do.

Most importantly, do it out of the kindness of your heart, not for your ego. There will always be bigger foundations and people who did it earlier. Be humble. Keep your head down and do the work. Keep politics and competition out of it at all costs. Keep your goal of helping people at the forefront, always.

What has stopped you from taking action to be a Better Human in the past?

My Lyme disease and co-infections can hinder or even stop my ability to be a Better Human. My days can go from good to bad easily, so I make sure I don't overwork myself. When I was younger, I thought that I might not be able to help enough because of my age, and I would lose courage. But now I realize that if I can help someone just a little bit, it's worth it. I often think about the boy and his mom living in their car because they sold their apartment to pay for medication. Even if I can help one person like them, it's enough. I know I can't cure someone of Lyme disease, but if I can ease someone else's pain - physically or financially - it will be worth it.

Tell me about a time when you failed trying to be a Better Human and what you did.

Being a Better Human is about widening your horizons and connecting with other people. A girl at my school had discovered my foundation and wanted to start one of her own. Hers was for a different cause, and she asked me how to start one. My first mistake was that I assumed she was trying to make fun of me, because that's what other classmates would have done. In middle school, a lot of people didn't react well when they learned of my disease. They were not used to people being different. Some people thought I was contagious and that something was immensely wrong with me. Once I realized that they just didn't understand it, I couldn't really blame them and I could block out the judgment and focus on my goals.

Once I realized this girl was serious about talking to me, I agreed to help. I gave her tips on how to create a strong non-profit organization, like making it unique from others, how it could become known, and how to mold it to accomplish her specific goals and who she wanted to help. I wanted to make sure she knew what she was getting into. And I wanted to make sure she was genuine. I didn't want her to just do it for likes on social media. It felt great to realize that I was helping her become a Better Human.

What's been your greatest challenge and how did you overcome that challenge to be a Better Human?

Peer pressure from classmates and adults has been very difficult for me over the years. From adults I hear "You're just a kid. You shouldn't be here." Some scientists and politicians brush me off. They passively aggressively tell me that it's not my place. In school, people would say that I was taking the money we raised for myself. They doubted if I was really doing the good things I said I was. When I applied to one school that I really wanted to go to, I was told that I would not be a good student there because of my activism. I was made to feel like I shouldn't be doing what I was.

It hurt at the time, but I realize now that they were empty comments and had nothing to back them up. I found a school that welcomed me and was so happy to have me. The principal's wife and son have Lyme disease. I feel really supported by everyone there. They're all about empowering women. It's been great so far.

Is there something/someone that inspires you to be a Better Human? What is it that inspires you?

I am inspired by the moms and dads who are still fighting for their children's health. I am inspired by the children, for putting on a smile during their worst days. They are the reason I started my organization.

Has your life changed as a result of being a Better Human? Tell me how.

I think that I have become more open to problems around the world instead of ignoring them. I also feel like I've mentally matured a few years throughout my journey. I've lost and gained many things, and met new friends along the way. I believe I got this disease for a reason, that I was recruited by a tick. And now I can help a community that needs it the most. If you ask me now, it sucks a lot, but I'm helping people. I've learned so many things and made so many connections. Who wants to be ordinary?! I wouldn't give it up. I didn't suffer through all of that for nothing. Now I have a purpose.

Tell me why young people can make a difference in the world if they take action.

Many people say that our generation will change the world. I believe it. I think we've seen the issues the world has, and we won't ignore them anymore. Our generation will change these issues because they've watched no one else do it.

Hillary's Reflections

Olivia's story is both heartbreaking and hope filled. It's hard to hear about children and their families having to fight through such difficult, sometimes seemingly hopeless, situations. As a parent, I found Olivia's story especially tough to hear. It's impossible to really understand what she and her family have experienced. 54 doctors. Stop for a moment and try to fathom the weight of that. I did my best in telling her story but I know there are countless details she glossed over because she has moved past them and is focused on the good she is doing now, as well as looking toward the future. And that's a wonderful thing.

To hear that she was bullied, mistrusted and dismissed while she was trying to save her own life and that of countless others is unimaginable. I, for one, am grateful that she had the maturity, resilience, and support of her family to rise above all of that. She is proving to all of those naysayers that she will never give up.

Olivia is a strong example of someone taking charge of their life. She has taken control of what she can and is doing everything she can to share her learnings with others. At an incredibly young age, she is doing more, changing more, achieving more, than most people will ever achieve in a lifetime. And she has no plans to slow down. To hear Olivia talk about her plans to travel around the world helping people with Lyme disease is awe inspiring. Let's just say the hair on my arms were standing up during most of my conversation with her!

Time to Reflect

The insights, passions, experiences and opinions we heard in our survey and interviews validated why we set out on this journey to write this book. We have been relentlessly taken aback by what people have shared and so grateful for what we have learned.

We fiercely hope that what we've presented in this book inspires you to think about what you care about, who you want to help, and to take action.

One of the questions we asked in our interviews was "What has stopped you from taking action to be a Better Human in the past?" We were very curious about what teens had to say because we believe most people want to be "good," but not everyone does something about it. So what stuff gets in the way?

In response to that question, we heard "fear of not fitting in," "fear of being rejected," "I thought I was too young," "I believed that I was just one person and couldn't make a difference." These responses weren't surprising, but they were comforting in a sense, because we all have probably felt these things in contemplating reaching out to someone. Even the most confident adult feels a little scared when they step up to do something out of the norm. Even adults fear that first step.

Believing we are all "Just one person and therefore can't make a difference" is an important reason people don't take action. It's important because it's DOWN RIGHT WRONG! We all may be "just one person" but WE DO MAKE A DIFFERENCE every time we interact with another human. We make a difference to them...to us...to the next person they come into contact with...even to others who are watching us. Think of it as a ripple effect. One caring act obviously impacts the person receiving it. Maybe it makes them smile at the next person they see, or puts a little skip in their step. Maybe it feels so good that they are driven to do something caring for someone else. And the recipient of *their* kind act goes on to do something wonderful for two more people. And those two people go on to do something caring for four people. You get the idea - one small act impacts far more than just that first person.

Now think about the people who see you do your caring thing. They're likely to be inspired to do the same.

Most teens we interviewed named their parents as being the ones who inspire them to be Better Humans. For some it was teachers, coaches, other teens. Kids watch their parents and they are inspired by what they see. That's a critically important message to parents. But if you are a teen and you are reading this, know that others are watching you; other teens, younger siblings, your friends, even your parents. You too can inspire others.

Oh, and remember our thoughts about selfless acts actually being *selfish*? Doing one compassionate act impacts YOU too, and makes you want to do it again and again! The ripple effect is endless!

We learned a ton from our data gathering and interviews. What we believe to be true is that it doesn't matter who you are, where you come from, how old you are, how much money you have, or who your parents are...you are incredible, you are of infinite value to this world and you have the power within you to make this world a better place. We can't wait to see what you do.

From our survey: complete list of words to describe what it means to be a Better Human

kind
respectful
empathetic
compassionate
helpful
thoughtful
caring
open-minded
open-hearted
honest
responsible
considerate`
engaged
generous
humble
understanding
forgiving
passionate
resilient
self-improving
accepting
brave
confident
courteous
giving
inspiring
leader

moral
supportive
unselfish
willing
ambitious
collaborative
cooperative
emotionally intelligent
encouraging
ethical
fair
friendly
good hearted
grateful
hard working
informed
knowledgeable
learner
mature
nice
patient
polite
positive
reliable
self-aware
selfless
smart

socially conscious
trustworthy
accommodating
accountable
active
adventurous
altruistic
appreciative
aware
better
calm
careful
celebrates differences
committed
communicative
connected
courageous
creative
curious
dedicated
dependable
determined
disciplined
driven
empowered
engaging
enterprising

environmentally conscious
evolved
exciting
fearless
financially literate
fun
growth
happy
inclusive
influential
insightful
inspired
intelligent
involved
joyful

just
life-balanced
listens
motivating
non-discriminatory
open to feedback
optimistic
persevering
perspective
planful
playful
proactive
productive
resourceful
risk-taker

self-control
self-respect
sharing
sincere
social
strong character
strong relationships
sympathetic
takes initiative
team player
tolerant of differences
visionary
volunteer
well rounded

Better Humans in Progress

Steve Brierley

I'm really a teenager at heart in adult clothes! Life is about adventure for me and trying something new every day is what gets me excited. I'm in if there is adrenaline involved! I love doing anything outdoors, but my main thrills are skiing, riding my single speed bike, riding my Triumph motorcycle or just being in the woods. I also like to push my body to the edge by doing Ironman Triathlons, Spartan Races or the Canadian Death Race (only did the Death Race once and didn't die!). I live by two mottos: "Anything is Possible if You Try" and "Give Back."

I try to be a Better Human everyday. Not always successful but it's always on my list of things to do.

I am a big believer in education and have a Master of Arts in Leadership, I'm an executive coach, a hobby writer and a lifelong learner.

THANKS for making this book possible.

Special thanks to all the people that let me go on, talking endlessly about writing this book. It gave me a chance to think out loud and validate whether my ideas were really sound or just nonsense.

Thanks to:

First and foremost, thanks to Alex Brierley, my partner in life and Perry Brierley, my son and social north star. Thanks for all the patience and understanding.

For guidance, continuous support and great listening skills:
Jason Grelowski
Karen Radford
Tom Morin - author of the book Your Best Work: Create The Working Life That's Right For You
Mark Frezell - author of the book Superpower: Release The Potential in Your Team
Murray Low
Special thanks to Perry, Riley, Reed, Izzy and Emily for your great stories.

Melissa From

Having spent most of my career in the charitable sector, I have had the privilege of seeing the best of humanity. I witness people giving of their time, talent and treasure every day and I am constantly inspired by the young people, volunteers and staff I work with.

I like to do random acts of kindness in small sneaky ways. I've been married to Derek for almost 20 years and we have two amazing kids, Sam and Ali. I am fueled by crazy amounts of coffee and bacon.

THANKS for making this book possible.

Thank you to the young people who indulged me and gave of your time for this project - Sahil, Sheliza, Paige, Amelia, and Zarek - you are all amazing!

I want to thank the amazing young people, volunteers and staff I have interacted with and been inspired by in my work with Junior Achievement over the last 10 years. It is such a privilege to work everyday with so many Better Humans.

All gratitude to my co-authors. Our shared passion for a better world brought us together and I feel so blessed to have taken this journey with you.

Mom and dad, every day you find ways to give back to your community. I have so many childhood memories of delivering meals to the elderly, picking up hitch-hikers, and just walking around the block to pick up garbage. You help me be a Better Human every day.

And finally, all of my love to Derek, Sam and Ali. I hope this book inspires you as much as it inspired me.

Paul Lamoureux

I joined the Better Human Group because I wholeheartedly believe that we all have a responsibility to be Better Humans and this is my way of leading the way. I'm a husband and a parent of two great kids and I want my family to see just how much of a difference they can make every day by doing just one simple act. I want my children to have the "How can I be better everyday?" mindset and live a life in which they make a difference and give back to our community.

I have a deep passion for helping kids be better and helping them plan their futures. This book reflects my commitment to making a difference in the lives of kids and it is a representation of all that I am. I hope that this book helps you see just how easy it can be to be a Better Human; we can all make a tremendous difference in the world.

They say we are the average of the 5 people we hang out with the most; I'm incredibly grateful for our team here at the Better Human Group. Being a part of this team simply makes me want to be better every day and I'm so excited for the future of our team. I'm especially grateful for Steve for being the driving force on this journey and inviting me to own a seat on the bus!

The definitive "why" for me to become a part of this team was our two children, Rory and Ryleigh. As a parent, I want our children to grow up with the mindset that we can all make a difference no matter how small that act may be. I want to teach them how to overcome their fears and make the world a better place. My wife Sheri has always been here to support whatever family adventure we have been a part of. I can't express enough appreciation and gratitude for my family - they are the most important people in my life, and my love for them is never ending.

A big "Thank You" goes out to those amazing teens who I was fortunate to interview for our book - Sarah, Owen, Katie, Adam and Markez. It was so empowering to see just how much one young teen can do when they simply decide to become better. I hope that those who read this book will be inspired and want to make a difference like they did.

Enjoy this book, share it with every teenager you know. We can't wait to see the difference it will make in your life.

Hillary Rideout

To me, being a Better Human means showing kindness and acting with compassion for others; being intentional about lifting others up. I am so excited to be a part of Better Human Group and writing this book! Through our work, I have found more meaning in my life and I am excited to share it. I am living a life of which I can be proud and to which my kids can look up.

Telling the stories of these incredible teens is my honour. I am truly inspired to live my life differently...to learn more, to empathize more, to act more.

My best friend and husband is Mike and I am beyond blessed to have had him next to me for 25 years. We have 2 children, Ben and Brooke, whom I love more than anything in the universe. They tell me they love me more, but we parents know that's impossible.

I owe my inspiration to be a Better Human to those around me. I surround myself with positive, compassionate people, and they drive me to be better. Thank you to my friends, family, and colleagues who talked with me throughout the process of gathering the data and stories for this book. Special gratitude for my friends Tara and Dave, who connected me to some of the most amazing teens appearing in this book.

To my children, Brooke and Ben - you are my greatest loves. You made me a mom and you make me proud every day. Now I want to inspire *you* and make *you* proud.

To my husband and best friend, Mike - thank you for always being in my corner, no matter what. Your support to me always, especially while working on this book, is so appreciated. Our conversations about what it means to be a Better Human inspired me more than you'll ever know.

To my mom, Wendy - you have inspired me for as long as I can remember. You are the kindest, most compassionate person I know, helping others every day. You inspire me and everyone who knows you.

Thank you to my Better Human Group partners - you are truly an inspiring group of Better Humans and I am honoured to work with you and call you my friends. A special thank you to Steve for seeing something inside me and inviting me to be a part of this amazing project.

Thank you to my tribe of lifelong friends and family - you are loyal, supportive and honest - I appreciate you more than you know.

To the brilliant teenagers I interviewed for the book - Ali, MacLean, Nick, Finley, Mason and Olivia - YOU ARE AN INSPIRATION - read that again and believe it. I will do what I can to have an impact on this world as you have. I will raise my children to do as you have. I am beyond inspired by your kindness, empathy and compassion for others, and absolutely thrilled to be helping to tell your stories.

Flip me over to find your very own call-to-action journal

CONGRATULATIONS!!!

If you're reading this, it means you've probably completed at least one of the things on the list of suggestions for how to be a Better Human or come up with something of your own.

The next step is to tell all your friends, neighbors, parents, teachers, or anybody who will listen, how great it felt to help others.

Please share this book or download the journal pages from our website at betterhumangroup.com.

Thank you for all you do to make this world a better place!

Better Human Journal

Record your **REFLECTIONS**
and **PLANS** here

5 What was the
impact on them?

6 What was the
impact on me?
What did I feel?

7 What am I planning next?

Better Human Journal

Record your **IDEAS**, your **INSPIRATION**, & your **ACTIONS** here

Date: _____

1 What will I do today to be a better human?

2 Who will I help today? Why them?

3 What do I hope to accomplish?

4 How will this make me a better human?

BETTER HUMAN
...in progress

Better Human Journal

Record your **REFLECTIONS**
and **PLANS** here

5 What was the
impact on them?

6 What was the
impact on me?
What did I feel?

7 What am I planning next?

Better Human Journal

Record your IDEAS, your INSPIRATION, & your ACTIONS here

Date: _____

1 What will I do today to be a better human?

2 Who will I help today? Why them?

3 What do I hope to accomplish?

4 How will this make me a better human?

Better Human Journal

Record your **REFLECTIONS**
and **PLANS** here

5 What was the
impact on them?

6 What was the
impact on me?
What did I feel?

7 What am I planning next?

Better Human Journal

Record your **IDEAS**, your **INSPIRATION**,
& your **ACTIONS** here

Date: _____

1 What will I do today to be a better human?

2 Who will I help today? Why them?

3 What do I hope to accomplish?

4 How will this make me a better human?

Better Human Journal

Record your **REFLECTIONS**
and **PLANS** here

5 What was the
impact on them?

6 What was the
impact on me?
What did I feel?

7 What am I planning next?

Better Human Journal

Record your IDEAS, your INSPIRATION,
& your ACTIONS here

Date: _____

1 What will I do today to be a better human?

2 Who will I help today? Why them?

3 What do I hope to accomplish?

4 How will this make me a better human?

Better Human Journal

Record your REFLECTIONS
and PLANS here

5 What was the
impact on them?

6 What was the
impact on me?
What did I feel?

7 What am I planning next?

Better Human Journal

Record your IDEAS, your INSPIRATION,
& your ACTIONS here

Date: _____

1 What will I do today to be a better human?

2 Who will I help today? Why them?

3 What do I hope to accomplish?

4 How will this make me a better human?

Better Human Journal

Record your REFLECTIONS
and PLANS here

5 What was the impact on them?

6 What was the impact on me? What did I feel?

7 What am I planning next?

Better Human Journal

Record your **IDEAS**, your **INSPIRATION**,
& your **ACTIONS** here

Date: _____

1 What will I do today to be a better human?

2 Who will I help today? Why them?

3 What do I hope to accomplish?

4 How will this make me a better human?

Better Human Journal

Record your **REFLECTIONS**
and **PLANS** here

5 What was the
impact on them?

6 What was the
impact on me?
What did I feel?

7 What am I planning next?

Better Human Journal

Record your **IDEAS**, your **INSPIRATION**, & your **ACTIONS** here

Date: _____

1 What will I do today to be a better human?

2 Who will I help today? Why them?

3 What do I hope to accomplish?

4 How will this make me a better human?

Better Human Journal

Record your **REFLECTIONS**
and **PLANS** here

5 What was the
impact on them?

6 What was the
impact on me?
What did I feel?

7 What am I planning next?

Better Human Journal

Record your **IDEAS**, your **INSPIRATION**, & your **ACTIONS** here

Date: _____

1 What will I do today to be a better human?

2 Who will I help today? Why them?

3 What do I hope to accomplish?

4 How will this make me a better human?

Better Human Journal

Record your **REFLECTIONS**
and **PLANS** here

5 What was the
impact on them?

6 What was the
impact on me?
What did I feel?

7 What am I planning next?

Better Human Journal

Record your **IDEAS**, your **INSPIRATION**, & your **ACTIONS** here

Date: _____

1 What will I do today to be a better human?

2 Who will I help today? Why them?

3 What do I hope to accomplish?

4 How will this make me a better human?

Better Human Journal

Record your **REFLECTIONS**
and **PLANS** here

5 What was the
impact on them?

6 What was the
impact on me?
What did I feel?

7 What am I planning next?

Better Human Journal

Record your IDEAS, your INSPIRATION, & your ACTIONS here

Date: _____

1 What will I do today to be a better human?

2 Who will I help today? Why them?

3 What do I hope to accomplish?

4 How will this make me a better human?

Better Human Journal

Record your **REFLECTIONS**
and **PLANS** here

5 What was the impact on them?

6 What was the impact on me? What did I feel?

7 What am I planning next?

BETTER HUMAN
...in progress

Better Human Journal

Record your IDEAS, your INSPIRATION,
& your ACTIONS here

Date: _____

1 What will I do today to be a better human?

2 Who will I help today? Why them?

3 What do I hope to accomplish?

4 How will this make me a better human?

Better Human Journal

Record your REFLECTIONS
and PLANS here

5 What was the impact on them?

6 What was the impact on me? What did I feel?

7 What am I planning next?

Better Human Journal

Record your IDEAS, your INSPIRATION,
& your ACTIONS here

Date: _____

1 What will I do today to be a better human?

2 Who will I help today? Why them?

3 What do I hope to accomplish?

4 How will this make me a better human?

Better Human Journal

Record your **REFLECTIONS**
and **PLANS** here

5 What was the
impact on them?

6 What was the
impact on me?
What did I feel?

7 What am I planning next?

Better Human Journal

BETTER HUMAN ...in progress

Record your IDEAS, your INSPIRATION, & your ACTIONS here

Date: _____

1 What will I do today to be a better human?

2 Who will I help today? Why them?

3 What do I hope to accomplish?

4 How will this make me a better human?

Better Human Journal

Record your **REFLECTIONS** and **PLANS** here

5 What was the impact on them?

6 What was the impact on me? What did I feel?

7 What am I planning next?

Better Human Journal

Record your IDEAS, your INSPIRATION,
& your ACTIONS here

Date: _____

1 What will I do today to be a better human?

2 Who will I help today? Why them?

 3 What do I hope to accomplish?

4 How will this make me a better human?

Better Human Journal

Record your **REFLECTIONS**
and **PLANS** here

5 What was the
impact on them?

6 What was the
impact on me?
What did I feel?

7 What am I planning next?

Better Human Journal

Record your IDEAS, your INSPIRATION, & your ACTIONS here

Date: _____

1 What will I do today to be a better human?

2 Who will I help today? Why them?

3 What do I hope to accomplish?

4 How will this make me a better human?

Better Human Journal

Record your REFLECTIONS
and PLANS here

5 What was the impact on them?

6 What was the impact on me? What did I feel?

7 What am I planning next?

Better Human Journal

BETTER HUMAN ...in progress

Record your IDEAS, your INSPIRATION, & your ACTIONS here

Date: _____

1 What will I do today to be a better human?

2 Who will I help today? Why them?

3 What do I hope to accomplish?

4 How will this make me a better human?

Better Human Journal

Record your **REFLECTIONS**
and **PLANS** here

5 What was the
impact on them?

6 What was the
impact on me?
What did I feel?

7 What am I planning next?

Better Human Journal

Record your **IDEAS**, your **INSPIRATION**,
& your **ACTIONS** here

Date: _____

1 What will I do today to be a better human?

2 Who will I help today? Why them?

3 What do I hope to accomplish?

4 How will this make me a better human?

Better Human Journal

Record your **REFLECTIONS**
and **PLANS** here

5 What was the
impact on them?

6 What was the
impact on me?
What did I feel?

7 What am I planning next?

BETTER HUMAN
...in progress

Better Human Journal

Record your **IDEAS**, your **INSPIRATION**,
& your **ACTIONS** here

Date: _____

1 What will I do today to be a better human?

2 Who will I help today? Why them?

3 What do I hope to accomplish?

4 How will this make me a better human?

Better Human Journal

Record your **REFLECTIONS**
and **PLANS** here

5 What was the
impact on them?

6 What was the
impact on me?
What did I feel?

7 What am I planning next?

Better Human Journal

Record your IDEAS, your INSPIRATION,
& your ACTIONS here

Date: _____

1 What will I do today to
be a better human?

2 Who will I
help today?
Why them?

3 What do I hope to
accomplish?

4 How will this make me a better human?

Better Human Journal

Record your **REFLECTIONS**
and **PLANS** here

5 What was the
impact on them?

6 What was the
impact on me?
What did I feel?

7 What am I planning next?

Better Human Journal

Record your IDEAS, your INSPIRATION,
& your ACTIONS here

Date: _____

1 What will I do today to be a better human?

2 Who will I help today? Why them?

3 What do I hope to accomplish?

4 How will this make me a better human?

Better Human Journal

Record your **REFLECTIONS**
and **PLANS** here

5 What was the impact on them?

6 What was the impact on me? What did I feel?

7 What am I planning next?

Better Human Journal

Record your **IDEAS**, your **INSPIRATION**, & your **ACTIONS** here

BETTER HUMAN ...in progress

Date: _____

1 What will I do today to be a better human?

2 Who will I help today? Why them?

3 What do I hope to accomplish?

4 How will this make me a better human?

Better Human Journal

Record your **REFLECTIONS**
and **PLANS** here

5 What was the
impact on them?

6 What was the
impact on me?
What did I feel?

7 What am I planning next?

Better Human Journal

Record your IDEAS, your INSPIRATION,
& your ACTIONS here

Date: _____

1 What will I do today to
be a better human?

2 Who will I
help today?
Why them?

3 What do I hope to
accomplish?

4 How will this make me a better human?

Better Human Journal

Record your REFLECTIONS
and PLANS here

5 What was the
impact on them?

6 What was the
impact on me?
What did I feel?

7 What am I planning next?

Better Human Journal

Record your IDEAS, your INSPIRATION,
& your ACTIONS here

Date: _____

1 What will I do today to be a better human?

2 Who will I help today? Why them?

3 What do I hope to accomplish?

4 How will this make me a better human?

Better Human Journal

Record your **REFLECTIONS**
and **PLANS** here

5 What was the
impact on them?

6 What was the
impact on me?
What did I feel?

7 What am I planning next?

Better Human Journal

Record your IDEAS, your INSPIRATION,
& your ACTIONS here

Date: _____

1 What will I do today to be a better human?

2 Who will I help today? Why them?

3 What do I hope to accomplish?

4 How will this make me a better human?

Better Human Journal

Record your **REFLECTIONS**
and **PLANS** here

5 What was the impact on them?

6 What was the impact on me? What did I feel?

7 What am I planning next?

Better Human Journal

Record your IDEAS, your INSPIRATION,
& your ACTIONS here

Date: _____

1 What will I do today to be a better human?

2 Who will I help today? Why them?

3 What do I hope to accomplish?

4 How will this make me a better human?

Better Human Journal

Record your **REFLECTIONS**
and **PLANS** here

5 What was the
impact on them?

6 What was the
impact on me?
What did I feel?

7 What am I planning next?

Better Human Journal

Record your IDEAS, your INSPIRATION,
& your ACTIONS here

Date: _____

1 What will I do today to be a better human?

2 Who will I help today? Why them?

3 What do I hope to accomplish?

4 How will this make me a better human?

Better Human Journal

Record your **REFLECTIONS**
and **PLANS** here

5 What was the
impact on them?

6 What was the
impact on me?
What did I feel?

7 What am I planning next?

Better Human Journal

Record your IDEAS, your INSPIRATION,
& your ACTIONS here

Date: _____

1 What will I do today to be a better human?

2 Who will I help today? Why them?

3 What do I hope to accomplish?

4 How will this make me a better human?

Better Human Journal

Record your **REFLECTIONS**
and **PLANS** here

5 What was the
impact on them?

6 What was the
impact on me?
What did I feel?

7 What am I planning next?

Better Human Journal

Record your **IDEAS**, your **INSPIRATION**,
& your **ACTIONS** here

Date: _____

1 What will I do today to be a better human?

2 Who will I help today? Why them?

3 What do I hope to accomplish?

4 How will this make me a better human?

Better Human Journal

Record your **REFLECTIONS**
and **PLANS** here

5 What was the
impact on them?

6 What was the
impact on me?
What did I feel?

7 What am I planning next?

Better Human Journal

Record your IDEAS, your INSPIRATION, & your ACTIONS here

Date: _____

1 What will I do today to be a better human?

2 Who will I help today? Why them?

3 What do I hope to accomplish?

4 How will this make me a better human?

Better Human Journal

Record your **REFLECTIONS**
and **PLANS** here

5 What was the
impact on them?

6 What was the
impact on me?
What did I feel?

7 What am I planning next?

Better Human Journal

Record your **IDEAS**, your **INSPIRATION**, & your **ACTIONS** here

Date: _____

1 What will I do today to be a better human?

2 Who will I help today? Why them?

3 What do I hope to accomplish?

4 How will this make me a better human?

80. Make a donation to a worthy cause (it does not have to be a lot)
81. Put your phone away when in the company of others and keep it away
82. Put positive sticky notes in places where others will see them and be uplifted
83. Stop to talk to a homeless person
84. Write or tell your partner what you love about him or her
85. Say thank you to the janitor at your work, school, or gym
86. Drop off cat or dog food at an animal shelter
87. Make 2 lunches instead of 1 and give one away at work or school
88. Be patient, kind and gracious to the customer rep on the phone
89. Tell a police officer how much you appreciate him or her
90. Help retrieve your neighbour's garbage can from the curb after collection
91. Compliment a parent on their polite and well-behaved kids
92. Leave only positive comments and responses on social media
93. Share a friend's blog, business website or art on social media
94. Leave a box of tennis balls at the park with a sign that explains it is meant for dog owners to use to play with their dogs
95. Offer that old cell phone, laptop, TV, or computer to someone in need
96. Make a difference by donating funds to someone on Kiva, Kickstarter or GoFundMe
97. Recommend someone for a job opening
98. Donate blood
99. Carpool with someone
100. Pay for someone else's meal anonymously at a restaurant
101. Drop-off personal hygiene items or diapers at a local shelter

60. Give someone a thoughtful gift (it does not have to be expensive)
61. Help a driver in need fix a flat tire or in some other way
62. Give up a parking space to someone and park further away
63. Give up your place in line at the bank, grocery store, etc.
64. Send flowers to someone, just because
65. Plant a tree or a plant
66. Cook or buy some food for someone
67. Donate old clothes and stuff you do not need
68. Go to a neighbour's house and introduce yourself
69. Take your grocery cart back to the store after you are done
70. Bake cookies or a cake for someone
71. Forgive someone who wronged you in the past
72. Tip someone you wouldn't ordinarily tip
73. Tell your parents how much you love and appreciate them
74. Give something away on your local buy & sell
75. Offer to babysit for someone
76. Give someone an inspiring book
77. Donate books to the library
78. Pick up trash that you see
79. Call your grandparents to chat

40. Be present - ignore your phone during a family meal
41. Tell a joke to a friend
42. Hug your sibling and parents
43. Ask someone how they are doing and then stop and really listen
44. Have coffee with a senior
45. Carry someone's bags from the store
46. Ask a friend about their dreams for the future and encourage them
47. Tell an adult in your life how they've helped you grow
48. Donate old sports equipment to those in need
49. Sign up for a volunteer opportunity
50. Say YES to something new today
51. Share a joyful post on social media
52. Introduce yourself to someone you see every day
53. Surprise someone with a small gift from the heart
54. Recognize someone for making a difference in your life
55. Offer to help someone out today
56. Tell someone what and how much they mean to you
57. Tell someone about how you plan to be a Better Human
58. Write a positive recommendation for someone on LinkedIn, especially someone looking for work
59. Identify your favourite charity and find out how you can help their cause...and then do it

20. Send someone an ecard or message to cheer them up
21. Tag someone in a social media post about how they inspire you
22. Do a chore at home without being asked
23. Give your mom and dad a hug
24. Say "Good morning/afternoon" to a stranger
25. Empty the dishwasher without your parents asking you to
26. Volunteer
27. Let someone get in front of you in line
28. Be gracious with your time
29. Help someone with their homework
30. Compliment someone
31. Tell someone you appreciate them and why
32. Volunteer in your community
33. Write a thank you note to a teacher
34. Smile at a stranger
35. Do more work than you promised
36. Reach out to an old friend to see how they are doing
37. Pick up garbage on your next walk
38. Buy a friend a coffee and chat about the future
39. Help someone else achieve their goal

101 great ideas for how to be a Better Human Do it by yourself, with a friend or your team!

1. Shovel someone's driveway or offer to mow their lawn
2. Compliment a friend
3. Tell a parent/guardian how they inspire you
4. Do something nice for a sibling
5. Write a thank you note to a teacher who encourages you
6. Buy a coffee for someone
7. Smile at a stranger
8. Walk around your block and pick up garbage
9. Hold the door open for someone
10. Let someone go ahead of you in line
11. Give up your seat on the bus for someone else
12. Go through your closet and donate your old clothes to charity
13. Do a carwash with your friends and donate the proceeds
14. Do a bottle drive with your friends and donate the proceeds
15. Give someone a hug, who looks like they are having a bad day (with their permission)
16. Write a letter to a deployed soldier
17. Share your snack with someone
18. Buy a pack of gum and share all the pieces
19. Offer to babysit for free

it. At the end of the day, before you go to bed, complete the remaining journal questions for the day.

At the end of the 30 day plan, look back at your journal entries and see how you have grown - but don't stop there! Commit to a Better Human deed every day. When you have finished the full list of Ways To Be A Better Human Teenager, follow us on social media for more ideas {@BetterHumanGroupInc}. And visit us at www.BetterHumanGroup.com to print off more journal pages.

Time to Take Action!

Being better at anything takes time and effort. The best athletes train and practice. So do the best musicians and artists. There is a widely held belief that it takes as much as 10,000 hours to achieve mastery in any area. So, it stands to reason that it is going to take some time and practice to be a Better Human Teenager too.

The great news is that you have already taken the first step by getting this book.

This journal will take you through a 30-day plan for personal growth as you learn to consistently perform random acts of kindness for family, friends and strangers. This is where you will track your progress, your setbacks, your strategies for success, and your reflections.

To get you started, we have curated a list of over 100 Better Human deeds. These range from simply smiling at a stranger to arranging a bottle drive for charity. Some of these suggestions might make you uncomfortable and might feel unnatural to you, but remember that the most growth will likely happen with the most discomfort.

Each day you should identify the Better Human deed that you are going to do that day. Write it in the journal and commit to

BETTER
HUMAN
JOURNAL

Better Humans in Progress
Steve Brierley, MA, CEC
Melissa From, CFRE
Paul Lamoureux, MA, CEC
Hillary Rideout, CPHR, BHRM

CPSIA information can be obtained
at www.ICGtesting.com
Printed in the USA
BVHW051503090321
602013BV00001BA/156